Mary E. Bradford, Company Barbour Brothers

A treatise on lace-making, embroidery, and needle-work with Irish flax threads

Mary E. Bradford, Company Barbour Brothers

A treatise on lace-making, embroidery, and needle-work with Irish flax threads

ISBN/EAN: 9783744738101

Printed in Europe, USA, Canada, Australia, Japan

Cover: Foto ©Andreas Hilbeck / pixelio.de

More available books at **www.hansebooks.com**

BARBOUR'S Prize Needlework Series

A Treatise on LACEMAKING EMBROIDERY and NEEDLEWORK with IRISH FLAX THREADS

Published by
THE BARBOUR
BROS. CO.

NUMBER SEVEN

Price Ten Cents

HIGHEST AWARDS - WORLD'S FAIR - 1893.

ESTABLISHED 1784.

Gold Medal Threads are the Best. Read the Record of Highest Awards.

STERLING AND FRANCINE CLARK ART INSTITUTE LIBRARY

BARBOUR'S THREADS HAVE STOOD THE TEST FOR MORE THAN A CENTURY.

THREAD WORKS:

PATERSON, NEW JERSEY. LISBURN, IRELAND. OTTENSEN, GERMANY.

STORES:

New York, 48 & 50 White St.
Chicago, 108 & 110 Franklin St.
Philadelphia, 410 Arch St.
Boston, 226 Devonshire St.
St. Louis, 717 & 719 Lucas Ave.
Cincinnati, 118 East 6th St.
San Francisco, 517 & 519 Market St.

Also in London, Manchester, Glasgow, Dublin, Paris, Hamburg, Montreal, Melbourne, Sydney, Brussels, Amsterdam, Madrid, Milan and Naples.

Forming collectively a Flax Thread industry employing 5000 persons or as large as any two other Linen Thread firms.

ASK FOR BARBOUR'S. INSIST UPON HAVING IT. SOLD EVERYWHERE.

BOOK NO. 7.

BARBOUR'S

PRIZE NEEDLE-WORK SERIES.

A TREATISE

ON

LACE-MAKING AND EMBROIDERY

WITH

PUBLISHED BY

THE BARBOUR BROTHERS COMPANY.

1900.

BOOKS No. 1, No. 2, No. 3, No. 4, No. 5, No. 6, AND No. 7,

ALSO

BOOK OF INSTRUCTION IN MACRAMÉ LACE-MAKING AND THE NEW ILLUSTRATED HANDBOOK OF TORCHON (OR BOBBIN) LACE-WORK,

will be sent to any address on receipt of ten cents each. In the Prize Needle-work Series no patterns are duplicated, and the whole form a compendium of the choicest designs.

If customers find difficulty in procuring Barbour's Irish Flax Threads and Flosses from their local stores, it will be sent from THE LINEN THREAD COMPANY, New York, postpaid, at prices below. We shall be pleased if our friends will kindly give, when writing, addresses of dealers to whom application for the threads has been made:

3-cord, 200-yards spools, dark-blue, white, whited-brown
(or écru), and drabs, spool . . . . 10 cents.
3-cord carpet thread, any color, skein . . . . 3 cents.
00 Ulster rope linen floss, 80 shades, skein . . . . . . 5 cents.
No. 4 etching flax, any color, 80 shades, 2 skeins . . . 5 cents.
Color book, containing full line of shades . . . . 10 cents.
White Star flossette, sizes *, **, ***, and ****, skein . . 5 cents.
New Irish flax lace threads, 3-cord, 200-yards spools, No.
120 and No. 150, spool . . . . 10 cents.
New Honiton lace thread, 2-cord, 200-yards spools, No.
250, very fine and strong, and serviceable also for the
finest knitting, crocheting, and other lace-work, spool, 10 cents.
Crochet thread, gray, écru, and white:
Nos. 16, 18, 20, and 25, ball . . . . 15 cents.
Nos. 30, 35, 40, and 50, ball . . . . 20 cents.
Nos. 60 and 70, ball . . . . 25 cents.
Flax macramé, 4-ounce ball . . . . 25 cents.
New Ulster (or Russian) braid, per yard, 5 cents; 12 yards, 50 cents.

Copyright, 1900,
by
THE BARBOUR BROTHERS COMPANY.

BOSTON
Rockwell and Churchill Press

CONTENTS.

1784  1900

AND again, to our friends and patrons in this and other lands, a hearty All-hail!

When No. 6 of the Prize Needlework Series was issued, meeting so eager a welcome from ladies everywhere, we had no thought that No. 7 would not follow it in the regular course of issue. During 1898, however, important changes in business methods and location took place, requiring the closest attention of the Barbour Brothers Company, — changes which while advantageous to the manufacturers of linen threads and flosses, are quite as much so to the great purchasing public served with these products. By and through the changes referred to has come a saving in rents and minor details, and in labor, — always to be favorably considered, since useless labor is a waste, — as well as a more extended application of the very latest improvements in machinery, all combining to facilitate the production of the best possible goods at the lowest possible prices.

So it is not until the dawn of the new century that No. 7 makes its appearance; an auspicious time, truly. Many have been disappointed at not receiving it earlier, but we trust the value of the book will render full compensation for the waiting. It comes just in time to aid in the preparation of Easter gifts, giving hints to busy brains and fingers during the long winter evenings yet to be, and later will prove a useful and pleasant companion through vacation days, when the wiser among women are making ready their offerings for the holiday season — even though this be months away. Just here we are tempted to give all our friends the benefit of a suggestion made by a valued correspondent who has awaited with exemplary patience the appearance of No. 7: "I was so disappointed not to receive the book before going to the mountains, last summer," she writes. "My vacation is spent in the preparation of gifts, which go into my Christmas-box to await the time for presentation. In this way I find much enjoyment myself, and cannot help believing that the gifts are of far more value to my friends if produced in an atmosphere of peace, quiet, and kindly thought, than if I must hurry and worry and fret over them at the last moment. I always take my Barbour books with me, and have to thank them for many beautiful and useful things. In fact, they have solved the question, 'What shall I give?' for me so completely and so many times that I am coming to look on them, one and all, as perfect treasure-boxes. The beauty of it is, too, that the articles described are so practical and useful, as well as ornamental; and the descriptions of them invariably give us some new idea that we may almost consider original! In themselves, with their beautiful print, paper, and illustrations, the books make most acceptable gifts for friends who are fond of needleworking. After this encomium can there be any doubt that I am anxiously awaiting No. 7? I do hope to have it in season for use during my summer outing."

Another: "I notice that suggestions are invited. Permit me to say that I find the 'Arlington Lace,' on page 33, book No. 3, an especially beautiful trimming for albs. The fact that the width may be varied as required for different uses is much in its favor."

Still other correspondents have asked that the books be devoted entirely to one or another class of work, but this seems hardly practicable. There is no kind of needlework in which the Irish flax products may not be used to the greatest advantage; and while we are glad to give extra space and attention to that which seems best understood and most popular with the majority, it would be hardly fair to devote the entire book of any year to this or any one class. Many correspondents write that often a single pattern is worth the price of the book, and this may well be true. A lady who does beautiful work with the crochet-needle states that she has made and sold nearly one hundred centre-pieces, as illustrated on page 23, book No 6. She says: "Made of Barbour's Irish flax thread, No. 25, this piece has the effect of carved ivory. Words cannot do it justice."

A little confusion seems to have arisen in the minds of some ladies concerning the terms "linen" and "flax." Linen thread is flax thread — made from the fibres of this plant after a wonderful process of manufacture. The story of its evolution from field to finished product — to the soft, lustrous flosses used in embroidery, the strong, smooth thread employed in lace-making, glove and harness stitching, carpet-sewing, book-binding, and every branch of industry in which thread or twine is used — is an intensely interesting one which cannot be more than hinted at here. The best flax, of long, strong, flexible fibre, comes from certain parts of Ireland. It is the use of this that gives the name to Barbour's Irish flax thread. Ladies are referred to page at the back of this book, which contains facsimiles of the spool, ball, carpet-thread and floss labels.

Our past policy regarding the Prize Needlework Series is to be continued. We are glad always to examine work done with Barbour's Irish flax threads and flosses, and to purchase such articles as are deemed suitable for publication. Directions, uniform with those printed in our books, must be carefully written out, the price plainly marked upon each article, and charges fully prepaid. Payment will be made upon acceptance. If not accepted, the article will be returned, transportation paid. Original work will receive especial attention. If not original, contributors will kindly state from what source the design submitted was obtained. The quantity of thread required for a yard of lace, or the length of lace made by one spool of thread, should be designated, together with the number of thread and the size or number of needles.

We will gladly make sale of work if possible. Kindly state, when sending articles to be sold, how long they shall be retained. Return charges on work intended merely for sale, and not submitted with a view to possible publication, must be paid by the owner.

We hope during the coming year to establish a salesroom devoted to the exhibition and sale of work done with the Irish flax products. Due notice of this will be given all desiring it. Realizing how many there are all over our country who need to add a little to their own personal incomes, and who cannot go from home for this purpose, it is our aim to aid ladies in disposing of their handiwork at prices which shall be fair to both purchaser and worker. A price-list of working patterns used in the prize Needlework Series has been prepared, and will be sent any lady desiring it, together with a table of contents for the entire series.

In return, we hope that our friends will recommend our books and the Irish flax threads to others who may not know of them, and that when writing they will inclose names of ladies who are interested in lace-work or embroidery, thus aiding us to make new friends continually. Rest assured, the favor will be appreciated.

MARY E. BRADFORD.

All communications should be addressed,

THE LINEN THREAD COMPANY,
Needlework Department,
48–50 White St., New York.

EXPLANATION OF TERMS AND ABBREVIATIONS USED IN BARBOUR'S PRIZE NEEDLE-WORK SERIES.

TERMS USED IN KNITTING.

K, knit plain.

O, over; thread over needle, forming an extra stitch. O 2, over twice.

N, narrow; knit two stitches together.

P, purl (or seam); knit with thread before needle.

Sl, n, and b, slip, narrow, and bind; slip first stitch, narrow next two, and draw slipped stitch over.

Sl and b, slip and bind; same as sl, n, and b, omitting the narrowing. To cast or bind off, continue the process.

Stars and parentheses indicate repetition; thus, * o 2, n, repeat from * twice, and (o 2, n,) 3 times, mean the same as o 2, n, o 2, n, o 2, n.

TERMS USED IN CROCHETING.

Ch, chain; a straight series of loops, each drawn with the hook through the one preceding it.

Sc, single crochet; hook through work, thread over and draw through work and stitch on hook at same time.

Dc, double crochet; hook through work, thread over, and draw through, over, and draw through two stitches on hook.

Tc, treble crochet; over, draw thread through work, over, draw through two stitches on hook, over, and draw through remaining two.

Stc, short treble crochet; like treble, save that the thread is drawn through the three stitches at once.

Dtc, double treble crochet; thread over twice before insertion of hook in work, then proceed as in treble crochet.

P, picot; a loop of chain joined by catching in first stitch of chain.

Complete illustrated directions for these stitches are given in "No. 1" of the Prize Series.

LACE MAKING AND EMBROIDERY.

ALPHABET LACE.

[Contributed by EVA M. STANIFORD, Thwing Terrace, Boston, Mass.]

Materials: Barbour's Irish flax thread, No. 80, 3-cord, 200-yards spools, and steel hook, size 000.

Ch 67 sts, turn.

1. Miss 7, 3 tc in next 3 sts, * ch 2, miss 2, a tc in next (forming a space), repeat from * 14 times, 3 tc in next 3, * miss 2, 3 tc each separated by 2 ch in next, repeat from * twice, or as many times as desired for depth of border; turn.

2. Ch 6, dc under 1st 2 ch, ch 3, dc under next 2 ch, ch 3, dc under next, ch 3, dc under next, ch 3, dc under next, ch 3, dc under next, ch 1, 4 tc in 4 tc, * 2 sp, 4 tc, 9 sp, 4 tc, 2 sp, * tc on tc, ch 2, tc in 3d of 7 ch; turn.

3. Ch 5, tc on tc, 2 sp, * 7 tc, 2 sp, 4 tc, 1 sp, 4 tc, 2 sp, 7 tc, 2 sp, * 4 tc in 4 tc, 3 tc each separated by 2 ch under each ch of 3 over middle tc of 1st row; turn.

4. Like 2d row to *, 2 sp, 34 tc, like 2d row from 2d * to end.

5. Like 3d to *, 1 sp, 28 tc, 3 sp, like 3d from 2d * to end.

6. As the beginning and ending of rows are the same as 2d and 3d, alternating, only directions for letters need be given; 2 sp, 7 tc, 3 sp, 4 tc, 2 sp, 10 tc.

7. 2 sp, 7 tc, 2 sp, 10 tc, 3 sp, 4 tc, 2 sp.

8. 5 sp, 7 tc, 1 sp, 4 tc, 2 sp, 7 tc.

9. 2 sp, 10 tc, 10 sp.

10. 9 sp, 10 tc, 3 sp.

11. 2 sp, 7 tc, 11 sp.

This completes the letter "F." Make 2 rows of sps between letters, and 3 or 4 rows between words. Any scallop or edge may be added that is liked, and the alphabet be used in a great variety of combinations. For a "Christmas apron" lace one might work the wish "A Merry Christmas," or the name of the one to whom the apron is to be presented. For a baby's pillow the words, "Sleep, Little One, Sleep," surrounded by a vine or other border, would be very appropriate, for a sofa-pillow cover, "Rest Here Thy Weary

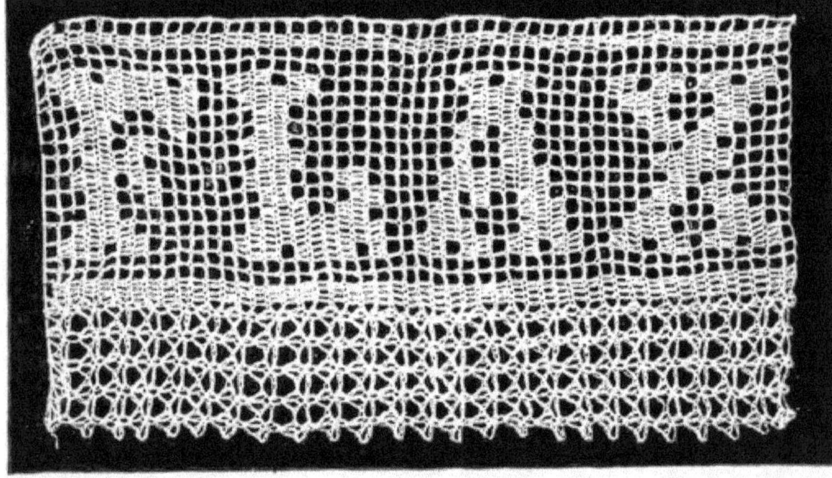

Alphabet Lace.

Head," etc. A very patriotic lady of my acquaintance has made a "Remember the Maine" lace for her sideboard scarf. In short, variations are endless, and with the word given ladies will find little difficulty in producing others. This word is also a suggestion of thread to be used, as no one after making lace with Barbour's linen (or Irish flax) thread will choose any other.

PICOT POINT LACE.

[Contributed by Miss C. A. Ragotzky, 2252 N. Twenty-first Street, Philadelphia, Pa.]

Materials: Barbour's Irish flax thread, No. 50, 3-cord, 200-yards spools (or finer, if desired), and steel hook, size 0. A spool makes 15 points, nearly a yard.

Ch 28 sts, turn.

1. A k-st, dc in 7th of ch, 2 k-sts, dc in next 4th st, 1 k-st, (5 tc in next 4th st) 3 times, 1 k-st, dc in 4th st, 1 k-st, 5 tc in 4th st, turn.

2. Ch 4, 5 tc in 1st tc, 5 tc in last tc, 1 k-st, dc in 1st st of next st, ch 3, a tc in each of next 4 tc, keeping last st of each on hook and drawing all off together, ch 1, tight, work down side of last tc made with sc to 1st st of next sh, and repeat, finishing next 2 diamonds in same way, working down last tc, 2 k-sts, fasten with a

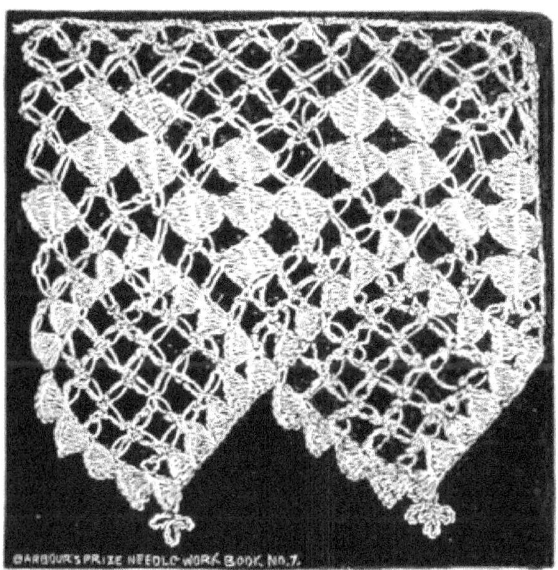

Picot Point Lace.

dc close to dc between 2 k-sts of last row, a dc close to same dc on other side, 2 k-sts, dc in ch at end of row, turn.

3. Ch 5, 1 k-st, fasten (as directed in last row; if preferred, simply make a dc in centre of dc between k-sts, but this method gives it more the appearance of the "Solomon's knot" in macramé), 2 k-sts, fasten, 2 k-sts, dc in centre of diamond, 1 k-st, 5 tc in centre of next diamond, 1 k-st, dc in centre of next, 1 k-st, 5 tc in

1st tc of next sh, 1 k-st, dc between shs, 1 k-st, sh (of 5 tc) in top of 4 ch of last row, turn.

4. Ch 4, sh in 1st tc, 1 k-st, dc in last tc, 2 k-sts, dc in 1st tc of next sh, 1 k-st, sh in last tc, 1 k-st, finish diamond as directed in 2d row, (2 k-sts, fasten) 3 times turn.

5. Ch 5, 1 k-st, fasten, 1 k-st, * sh in dc between next k-sts, repeat from *, 1 k-st, dc in top of diamond, 1 k-st, sh in 1st tc of next sh, 1 k-st, dc in last tc, (2 k-sts, fasten) twice, 1 k-st, sh in last tc of sh, turn.

6. Ch 9, dc in 6th (from hook), ch 6, dc in same, ch 6, dc in same, 5 tc in 1st tc of sh, 1 k-st in last tc, (2 k-sts, fasten) 3 times, 1 k-st, sh in last tc of sh, 1 k-st, finish 2 diamonds as in 2d row, 2 k-sts, fasten, turn.

7. Ch 5, 1 k-st, fasten, 1 k-st, (sh in top of diamond) twice, 1 k-st, dc in 1st tc of next sh, 1 k-st, sh in last tc, 1 k-st, fasten, (2 k-sts, fasten) twice, 1 k-st, sh in 1st tc of last sh, turn.

8. Sc in each tc of sh, ch 4, sh in same tc, 1 k-st, fasten, 2 k-sts, fasten, 1 k-st, sh in 1st tc of next sh, 1 k-st, dc in last tc, 2 k-sts, finish 2 diamonds as directed in 2d row, 2 k-sts, fasten in ch at end, turn.

9. Ch 5, 1 k-st, fasten, (2 k-sts, dc in top of diamond) twice, 1 k-st, sh in dc between next 2 k-sts, 1 k-st, dc in 1st tc of sh following, 1 k-st, sh in last tc, 1 k-st, fasten, 1 k-st, sh in 1st tc of sh, turn.

10. Sc in each tc, ch 4, sh in same tc, sh in 1st tc of next sh, 1 k-st, dc in last tc of sh below, 2 k-sts, finish diamond, (2 k-sts, fasten) 3 times, turn.

A very rich and handsome design for finishing a sideboard scarf. In finer flax thread it may be used for many purposes.

IVY LACE.

[Contributed by Mrs. M. M. MOTT, 89 Washington Street, Morristown, N.J.]

Materials: Barbour's Irish flax thread, No. 60, 3-cord, 200-yards spools, and steel hook, size 0.

Ch 70 st; turn.

1. Miss 7, 4 tc in 4 st, * ch 2, miss 2, a tc in next, repeat from * 13 times, forming 14 spaces, 3 tc in next 3 st, ch 2, miss 2, a tc in next, * 2 tc separated by 2 ch in next st, miss 2, repeat from last * to form 4 loops in all; turn.

Ivy Lace.

2. Ch 3, * 3 tc, 1 ch and 1 tc under 2 ch, repeat 3 times, tc in tc, ch 2, 4 tc in 4 tc, * ch 2, tc in next tc, repeat 4 times, 12 tc in next 12 st, ch 2, miss 2, 13 tc in next 13 st, ch 2, miss 2, 4 tc on 4 tc, ch 2, miss 2, tc in next; turn.

3. Ch 5, 4 tc on 4 tc, ch 2, miss 2, 13 tc in next 13 st, * ch 2, miss 2, 13 tc in next 13 st, ch 2, tc on tc, repeat 3 times, 3 tc on next 3 tc, * ch 2, tc on tc, 2 tc separated by 2 ch under each 1 ch of last row; turn.

4. Like 2d row to 2d *; 4 sp (2 tc separated by 2 ch), 13 tc in 13 tc, 1 sp, 13 tc in 13 tc, 1 sp, 4 tc in 4 tc, ch 2, tc in 3d st of 5 ch; turn.

5. Ch 5, 4 tc in 4 tc, 2 sp, 10 tc on last 10 of 13 tc, 1 sp, 10 tc

on 10 tc, 1 sp, 7 tc (in last of 13 tc, and on 2 sp following), 2 sp, 4 tc on 4 tc, finish like 3d row from 2d *.

6. Like 2d row to 2d *; 1 sp, 13 tc, 3 sp, 4 tc, 5 sp, 4 tc, ch 2, and tc in 3d of 5 ch; turn. The tc helping to form last sp is counted.

7. Ch 5, 4 tc in 4 tc, 2 sp, 10 tc, 1 sp, 4 tc, 2 sp, 13 tc, 1 sp, 4 tc; like 3d row from 2d *.

8. Like 2d row to 2d *; 2 sp, 10 tc, 1 sp, 4 tc, 2 sp, 13 tc, 1 sp, 4 tc, ch 2, tc in 3d of 5 ch; turn.

9. Ch 5, 4 tc in 4 tc, 1 sp, 13 tc, 3 sp, 4 tc, 5 sp, 4 tc; like 3d row from 2d *.

10. Like 2d row to 2d *; 2 sp, 10 tc, 1 sp, 10 tc, 1 sp, 7 tc, 2 sp, 4 tc, ch 2, tc in 3d of 5 ch; turn.

11. Ch 5, 4 tc, 4 sp, 13 tc, 1 sp, 13 tc, 1 sp, 4 tc; like 3d row from 2d *.

12. Like 2d row to 2d *; 1 sp, 13 tc, 1 sp, 13 tc, 4 sp, 4 tc, ch 5, tc in 3d of 5 ch; turn.

13. Ch 5, 4 tc, 5 sp, 7 tc, 3 sp, 7 tc, 2 sp, 4 tc; like 3d row from 2d *.

14. Like 2d row to 2d *; 14 sp, 4 tc, ch 2, tc in 3d of 5 ch; turn. Repeat from 2d row. This trimming will be found especially suitable for pillow-slips, aprons, etc., in the finer thread, while in No. 40 or No. 50 of Barbour's Irish flax thread, either white, gray, or ecru it is very handsome for finishing the ends of sideboard or dresser scarfs. The insertion is made by leaving off the lower edge of shs.

LACE FOR SIDEBOARD SCARF.

[Contributed by Mrs. A. L. WERTMAN, Tannersville, Pa.]

Materials: No. 30 Barbour's Irish flax thread, and steel hook, size 0.

The principal parts of this handsome design are made up of a new and original stitch, first appearing, with complete directions for working it, in Barbour's Prize Needlework Series, No. 6. It is called the spoke, or Russian stitch, as it resembles some Russian work. Ch 7, join.

1. Ch 10, * take a loop around the ch, thread over, draw through, repeat from * 19 times, keeping all on hook, take a loop through ring, thread over, draw through all loops on hook, drawing tight enough to curve the stitch; let this loop on the needle remain idle; that is, do not work through it until called for. With the hook draw a loop through ring, ch 5, draw last ch through idle loop on hook, ch 5, and repeat from *, making 10 loops on each 5 ch. Work 8 curved spokes as described, joining last to first at back.

2. Draw thread to top of spoke from joining (if preferred, the thread may be cut and joined in), ch 6, * 4 dtc with 3 ch between in top of next spoke (about 3 loops from the end), ch 3, tc in next spoke, ch 3, repeat from * 3 times, and join to 3d of 6 ch.

Lace for Sideboard Scarf.

3, 4, 5, 6. Dc in each st, with 3 dc in each corner st; turn at end of row, forming ribs, as described for table-mats in No. 5. As all are doubtless familiar with the method, it is not necessary to describe it.

7. Tc separated by 2 ch all around, with 3 tc in corners.

8. Ch 7, 12 loops on ch, catch in space and draw through, working exactly as described for centre, except that there are 4 ch for lower part and 3 for upper part of spokes, with 5 loops on the 3

ch, and 7 on the 5; fasten in the spaces, making 1 or 2 dc to suit fulness. A little practice is all that is required, as the work is very simple.

9. The small wheels between the squares are made like centre of the latter. Join squares corner to corner by 3 spokes, when working, or with needle and thread, as preferred. Begin at 4th spoke on corner of 1st square, fasten in, ch 6, fasten in spoke of small wheel, ch 6, miss 1 spoke of square, fasten, ch 6, fasten in next spoke of wheel, ch 6, miss 1 spoke of square, fasten in next, ch 12, miss 1 spoke, fasten in next, * ch 5, fasten in next, 4 times, work opposite side of square like first, taking 2d wheel, ch 6, fasten in corresponding spoke of next square, and repeat to length of lace.

10. Fasten in top of 1st upper spoke of wheel, ch 5, fasten in next, ch 5, thread over 5 times, a dtc under 12 ch, catch in top of 3d spoke of wheel, work off remaining st, ch 5, a dtc under same 12 ch, ch 5, tc under 5 ch, ch 4, dc under next, ch 4, dc under next, ch 4, dc under next, ch 4, tc under next, ch 5, thread over 5 times, dtc in 1st unoccupied spoke of next wheel, catch in centre of 12 ch, work off remaining st, ch 5, and repeat from first of row.

11. Tc, with 2 ch between.

12, 13. Dc in each st.

14. Tc in 1st st, * ch 3, tc in top of tc just made, miss 2 st, tc in next, and repeat.

The squares may be used for tidies or joined for any purpose desired. The lace would be beautiful for finishing a centre-piece, as a corner may be nicely turned, and for this purpose should be made of No. 50 Barbour's Irish flax thread.

FLORIDA SHELL LACE, FOR HANDKERCHIEF.

[Contributed by SATIE J. CAMPIN, Orlando, Florida.]

Materials: Barbour's Irish flax lace thread, No. 250, 2-cord, 200-yards spools, steel hook size 000, or the finest you can obtain, a yard of Honiton insertion, and 8-inch square of fine linen lawn. Any size desired may be used for the centre, but the smaller the daintier. The lace edge, complete, is 3 inches wide, but may be narrower if preferred.

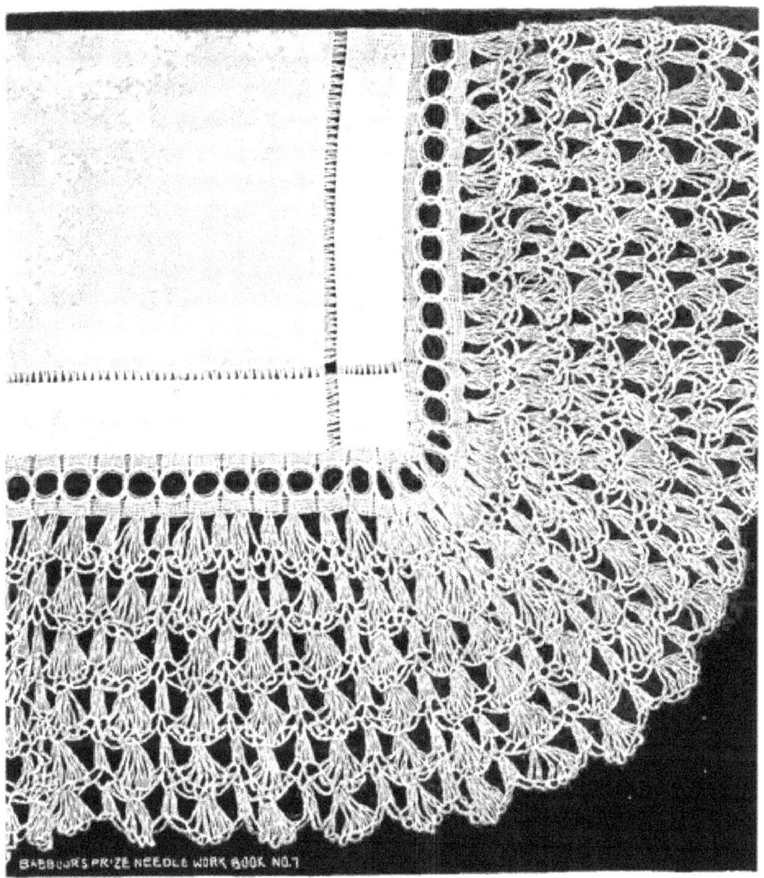

Florida Shell Lace, for Handkerchief.

Draw 6 threads one inch from edge of lawn, all around, turn hem neatly and hemstitch. Width of hem may, of course, be left to one's own taste. Sew the insertion around this square, fulling at the corners. Begin lace by drawing thread through outer edge of insertion and fastening well. The 1st row of shs is made around the insertion about ¼ inch apart; no exact rule can be given for this, as there are no picots on the edge. Simply make the shs even, and not too full. Fasten in near a corner:

1. Ch 3, 3 tc in same place,* ch 1, miss a space, sh of 6 dtc each separated by 1 ch, ch 1, miss a space, smaller sh of 4 tc, and repeat from *. In the large shells draw the middle stitches up longer; all should be drawn out longer than ordinarily and worked quite loose, to give the fluffy, dainty appearance. The shells should be made a trifle nearer together at the corners. Also arrange to have them come out even, so that 2 large or 2 small ones will not come together. This can easily be done by a little calculation when near the end. Join last 1 ch to top of 1st 3 ch.

2. Make 2 sc along top of 1st small sh, fastening between 2 tc, * ch 6, fasten between 1st and 2d dtc, of large sh, (ch 5, fasten between next 2,) 4 times, ch 6, fasten between 2d and 3d tc of small sh, and repeat from *, fastening last 6 ch where 1st started.

3. Work back in sc to middle of 6 ch just made, * ch 5, fasten in middle of next 6 ch, ch 6, fasten in 2d loop of 5 ch, ch 5, fasten in next loop, ch 6, fasten in middle of 6 ch following, and repeat from *, joining where started.

This completes the sh. Repeat from 1st row, beginning with a single under 5 ch, and ch 3 for 1st tc. Make shs in the loop exactly over shs of previous row. Three rows constitute a sh, and as many shs may be made as desired for the border. The sample has 6, requiring 1½ spools of thread. I cannot speak too highly of the lace thread for work of this nature; it is so silken, yet crisp and dainty. Barbour's Irish flax I have found superior to all thread for lace-work, and am sure ladies will "take no other" after giving this a trial.

TABLE OR TOILET MATS.

[Contributed by Miss ANNA HARRIS, 1103 Corning Street, Red Oak, Iowa.]

Materials: Two and one-half spools of Barbour's Irish flax thread, No. 40, white, 3-cord, 200-yards spools, crochet hook size 1, and ¼ yard of heavy butcher's linen, for centres.

First mark the centres on the linen, of any shape and size desired. The set of which one is illustrated has two oval mats, one large round mat, and two small round ones. The largest oval centre is 7 × 4½ inches, the smaller is 6 × 4 inches; the large round centre is 6 inches in diameter, and the smaller ones 4½ inches. First, buttonhole the edges all around, over the pencil line, — and it is a good plan to stitch around this, to make a firmer edge, — using 2 short and 1 long stitch. For the border:

Table or Toilet Mats.

1. Fasten in, ch 3, and make a tc in every buttonhole stitch all around, joining to top of 3 ch by a single.

2. Ch 4, * miss 1, a tc in next, ch 1, repeat from * all around, joining to 3d of 4 ch.

3. Ch 8, turn, a dc in each stitch of ch, * ch 1, turn, a dc in

each of 8 dc, repeat from * 5 times, forming a solid square, miss 2 tc of last row, a triple tc (thread over 3 times) in next, ch 8, miss 2 tc, a sc in next, ch 6, a tc in 3d stitch of 8 ch, ch 2, a tc in 6th stitch, ch 2, a tc in top of triple tc, ch 6, turn, tc in tc, in each of 2 ch and in next tc ch 2, tc in 3d of 6 ch, ch 6, turn, tc in tc, ch 2, miss 2, tc in tc, ch 2, miss 2, tc in 3d of 6 ch, turn, and work along edge of square with sc to lower corner, miss 2 tc below, a triple tc in next, and repeat from beginning of row, alternating solid and open squares, and joining corner of last to 1st by 1 sc.

4. Ch 5, * a dtc in 2d row of square, ch 2, a tc in 5th row, ch 2, 2 tc separated by 2 ch in corner, ch 2, miss 3, a tc, ch 2, miss 3, a dtc, a triple tc in top of triple tc below, work around open square in same way, and repeat from * around mat, joining last dtc to top of 5 ch.

5. Catch back with a dc under 2 ch last made, * ch 5, a dc under 1st 2 ch of next square, ch 3, a dc under next 2 ch, ch 1, a tc under next 2 ch, (ch 7, fasten back in 1st stitch to form a picot, ch 1, a dtc under same 2 ch) 4 times, p, ch 1, a double under 2 ch, ch 3, a dc under next 2 ch, and repeat from beginning of row. If preferred, the 1st and last of each scallop may be trebles.

If a heavy linen duck is used these make very durable table-mats. A coarser number of thread may be used, if preferred, but No. 40 makes a lovely, rich, and heavy border in this pattern.

SQUARE FOR BEDSPREAD.

[Contributed by ESTELLE BALL, Talmage, Kansas.]

Materials: Barbour's Irish flax thread, No. 30, 3-cord, 200-yards spools, and steel hook, size 1.

1. Wind thread 10 times around a large lead-pencil, slip off and fasten with 1 double; ch 4, 7 dtc in ring, * ch 7, 8 dtc in ring, repeat from * twice, ch 7 and join to top of 4 ch.

2. Ch 3, 1 tc in every st all around, with 3 in corners, to widen; join to top of 3 ch.

3. Ch 5, a tc in same place, miss 2, 2 tc separated by 3 ch in

next, repeat around block, at the corners making 3 tc in a st, with 3 ch between each. Join to 3d of 5 ch.

4. Like 3d row, making sh in sh, same at corners.

5. Sh in sh, 5 tc in next sh, 3 shs, 5 dtc between shs at corner, 3 shs, 5 tc, and so continue.

6. Ch 3, 4 tc in sh, * ch 4, 5 tc in next sh, sh in each of next 2 shs, 8 tc separated by 5 ch at corner (put 1 tc on last tc of sh, 3

Square for Bedspread.

on dtc, ch 5, a tc in same place as last, 2 on dtc, 1 on tc), 2 shs in shs, 5 tc in next sh, and repeat from * all around, joining to top of 3 ch.

7. Catch back in previous sh, ch 3, 4 tc in same sh, * ch 5, a tc under 4 ch, ch 5, 5 tc in next sh, sh in next, 4 tc on 4 tc, ch 5, 1 tc in 3d st of 5 ch, ch 5, 4 tc in last 4 tc, missing 1st (counting tc of sh), sh in sh, 5 tc in next sh, and repeat around, joining to top of 3 ch.

8. Catch back as before, ch 3, 4 tc, * ch 5, 1 tc under next ch, ch 5, a tc under next, ch 5, 5 tc in next sh, miss 1 tc, 3 tc in next 3, ch 5, 5 tc in tc at corner, ch 5, miss 1 tc, 3 tc in next 3, 5 tc in sh, and repeat from *, joining to top of 3 ch.

9. Ch 8, * a tc under 5 ch, ch 5, 5 tc under next 5 ch, ch 5, a tc under next, ch 5, miss 3 tc, 4 tc in next 4, ch 5, 3 tc in 3 tc at corner, ch 5, 1 tc in same tc as last, 2 in next 2, ch 5, miss 1 tc, 4 tc in next 4, ch 5, and repeat from *, joining to 3d of 8 ch.

10. Catch back in preceding tc, ch 7, * a tc under 5 ch, ch 4, 5 tc under next 5 ch, ch 4, 5 tc under next 5 ch, ch 4, a tc under next, ch 4, miss a tc, 2 tc in next 2, ch 5, 3 tc in 3 tc, ch 5, a tc in centre of 5 ch, ch 5, 3 tc on tc, ch 5, 2 tc in centre of 4 tc, ch 4, and repeat from *, joining to 3d of 7 ch.

11. Ch 7, * 5 tc under next ch, ch 5, a tc under next, ch 5, 5 tc under next, ch 4, a tc in tc, ch 5, 3 tc in 3 tc, ch 5, 2 tc separated by 5 ch in tc at corner, ch 5, 3 tc in tc, ch 5, tc on 2d tc, ch 4, and repeat from *, joining to 3d of 7 ch.

12. Ch 3, a tc in every st all around, with 5 in corner st, to widen; join to top of 3 ch.

This completes the block. Join as follows: Ch 4, turn; shell of 3 tc, 2 ch, 1 tc in 1st st of ch, ch 2, fasten at corner of block, turn; shell under 2 ch in shell just made, ch 2, fasten to another block, and repeat. This design is very pretty for tidies. The connection may be of chains, thus: Fasten in 1st block, ch 10, fasten in 2d block, a single in next 3 tc, ch 10, fasten in 1st block, and so on. The 4th ch may be caught under preceding 2, thus: Ch 5, a sc under 2d ch below, ch 5, fasten in opposite block. Run ribbon in the spaces, over the single chains and under the triple ones. If desired, an extra row of dtc may be added to each block, separating each by 2 ch, the blocks joined by overseaming neatly, and narrow red and blue ribbon alternately run in the spaces. In these "patriotic" days, this suggestion will find favor. There is much pleasure in evolving new ideas, no less in the use of the linen threads for lace-work of any description, they are so rich and satisfactory in every way.

PLATE DOILY.

[Contributed by EMMA PETTIT, Grimsby, Ontario, Can.]

Materials: Barbour's Irish flax thread, ecru, No. 100, 3-cord, 200-yards spools, and steel hook, size 000.

Ch 12, join.

1. Begin each row with 3 ch for a tc, 36 tc in ring, join (always) to third stitch of chain.

Plate Doily.

2. A tc in every other stitch, 2 ch between.

3. 2 tc in 1 tc, 3 ch between.

4, 5, 6, 7, 8. Same as 3d row, increasing 1 tc each row. In 8th row there will be 7 tc on 6 tc, with 3 ch between.

9. 4 tc on 4 tc, ch 1, 4 tc on 4 tc, ch 3, repeat.

10, 11, 12, 13, 14, 15, 16, 17. Same as 9th row, increasing the ch between groups of 4 tc 1 stitch each row. The 17th row has 10 ch.

18. 4 tc in tc, ch 4, 2 tc in 5th and 6th of 10 ch, ch 4, 4 tc on tc, ch 3, repeat.

19. 4 tc on tc, ch 4, miss 3, 4 tc, ch 4, miss 3, 4 tc, ch 3, and repeat.

20. Missing 1st of 4 tc, 4 tc in 4 sts, ch 4, 2 tc in centre of 4 tc, ch 4, miss 4, 4 tc, ch 6; repeat.

21. 4 tc (missing 1st), ch 8, 4 tc (1st in ch, 3 in tc of last row), ch 3, 1 tc, ch 5, 1 tc, ch 3, all under 6 ch, ch 3, and repeat.

22. 4 tc (as in 21st row), ch 6, 4 tc, ch 3, 1 tc under 3 ch, ch 3, 1 tc under next loop, ch 5, 1 tc in same place, ch 3, 1 tc under 3 ch, ch 3; repeat.

23, 24. Like 22d row, decreasing ch in diamond by 2 sts each row, and increasing the loops, making 3 ch and 1 tc twice more every row.

25. 8 tc over 3 tc, 2 ch and 3 tc, 11 loops as directed, and repeat.

26. 4 tc in centre of 8 tc, missing 1st and last 2, ch 7, catch back into 5th from hook to form a p, ch 2, a tc under 3 ch, repeat in every loop, with 2 in centre loop, and continue around.

Made of coarser thread, No. 40 or No. 50 Barbour's Irish flax, this design makes a very handsome and serviceable cover for a piano stool, or tidy.

GENTLEMEN'S SUSPENDERS.

[Contributed by Miss ANNA FITCH, New Haven, Conn.]

Materials: Barbour's Irish flax thread, No. 25, 3-cord, 200-yards spools, and steel hook, size 2, or large enough to carry the thread smoothly, with 2 skeins Ulster rope linen or etching flax, blue, or any desired color. Two spools of thread are required. An afghan hook is best, but for so narrow a strip an ordinary hook may be used.

Ch 19 sts, turn.

1. Take up and draw thread through each consecutive st of ch, keeping all on the hook.

2. Thread over, draw through a st, * over, draw through 2 sts, and repeat until all are worked off. Repeat these 2 rows to the

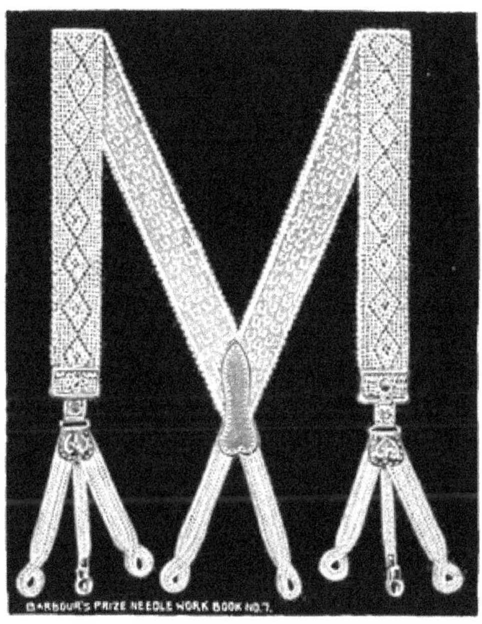

Gentlemen's Suspenders.

length of 27 inches, in the 3d row drawing up the sts under each little upright loop appearing on the surface of the work. This is the plain afghan or tricot st.

Having made 2 strips of length designated, proceed to embroider them in cross-stitch, or as desired. Cross-stitching is easily done on the afghan work. Use the rope linen if a simple design is chosen, or the etching flax if this is more elaborate. It is best to line the bands with a broad elastic slightly narrower than the work, felling this on with a finer linen thread firmly but easily, to allow the band to give a little with the elastic when worn, and not so closely that it may not be removed if necessary to launder the crocheted bands. For all such purposes linen thread is very suitable, having the silken lustre, and refusing to grow rough with service.

DOILY, IN ROLL AND KNOT STITCH.

[Contributed by ANNIE WILLIAMS, Steubenville, O.]

Materials: Barbour's Irish flax crochet and lace thread, in balls, or 3-cord, 200-yards spools, No. 40, steel hook, size 1, and circle of linen 6 inches in diameter.

Buttonhole around linen, using long and short st, again with short st. Fold linen three times, dividing it into eight sections. Cut a circle an inch in diameter and half an inch from edge from each section, buttonhole around with long and short st, and fill in with loose buttonhole st, or any desired. Divide the circumference of the linen into sections of three-fourths and half an inch alternately; this will given 16 of each.

1. Fasten in at beginning of half-inch space, make 6 roll-st of 24 overs each, 2 k-st, miss three-fourths inch, and repeat. Join last k-st to top of 1st roll, a dc between 1st and 2d roll-st, dc between 2d and 3d.

2. A roll-st in same place, 2 roll-st between 3d and 4th, 1 between 4th and 5th, 2 k-st, dc in dc between k-st of last row, 2 k-st, 4 roll-st in centre of 6 roll-st, as before, repeat around, and join.

3. 2 roll-st in centre of 4 roll-st, * 2 k-st, dc in dc of last row, repeat twice, and repeat from beginning of row.

4. A roll-st in centre of 2 roll-st, * 2 k-st, fasten, repeat 4 times, then repeat row, fastening in top of roll-st.

5. 10 roll-st in top of roll-st, fasten in dc between next k-st, * 2 k-st, fasten in next dc, repeat twice, then repeat row, catching in top of 1st roll-st.

6. A dc between 1st and 2d roll-st, * 2 k-st, dc between next 2, repeat 7 times, 1 k-st, fasten in next k (dc between k-st), 2 k-st,

fasten in next, 2 k-st, fasten in next, 1 k-st, and repeat row, joining last k-st where started.

7. A dc in next k, ch 3, tc in same, ch 2, 2 tc in same, * sh of 2 tc, 2 ch and 2 tc in next k, repeat 6 times, dc in next k, 2 k-st, fasten in next, sh in next, and repeat from *.

8. Sh of 7 tc under 2 ch in sh of last row, repeat 7 times, fasten in k, repeat row all around.

Doily in Roll and Knot Stitch.

A very handsome piece for any purpose required, especially for the top of small polished table, or taboret. The roll-st is accurately described in No. 4 Book, page 33.

HEXAGON DOILY.

[Contributed by Mrs. SARAH HALE, Romulus, Mich.]

Materials: Barbour's Irish flax thread, No. 80, 3-cord, 200-yards spools, and steel hook, size 000.

1. Ch 15, tc in 1st st, * ch 10, tc in same st, repeat 3 times, ch 5, dtc in 5th st of 15 ch.

2. Ch 8, and sc in top of ch loop; repeat.

3. Ch 3 for 1st tc, 9 tc under 1st 8 ch, 10 tc under each of 5 loops, making 2 ch between each group; join to top of 3 ch.

4. Ch 3, tc in tc, all around, with 1 tc, 2 ch, and 1 tc under 2 ch of last row; join to top of 3 ch.

5, 6, 7. Like 4th, with 2 tc, ch 2, and 2 tc under 2 ch at corners.

8. Ch 4, miss 1, * tc in next, ch 1, miss 1, repeat around, with 1 tc, 2 ch, and 1 tc under ch at corners; join.

9. Ch 3, tc in ch, tc in tc, repeat around, with 1 tc, 2 ch, and 1 tc in corner ch; join. This completes the centre, which may be made as much larger as desired.

Border: 1. Dc in 4 tc, ch 9, * sc in 5th st of 9 ch, ch 4, dc to corner, 1 dc, 2 ch, and 1 dc under corner ch, 15 dc in next 15 tc, ch 9, and repeat.

2. Ch 5, dc in loop of last row, ch 5, turn work, sl-st in last dc made, * ch 9, dc in loop, ch 5, sl-st in 5th st of 9 ch, repeat from * 6 times, miss 4 dc, dc in dc with 1 dc, 2 ch, and 1 dc in corner ch, 9 dc down other side, and repeat row.

3. 5 dc in each ch between loops, dc in dc with 1 dc, 2 ch, and 1 dc at corners.

4. Dc around loops, making 3 dc in 3d st between 4th and 5th loops, ch 7, 4 tc each separated by 2 ch under corner ch, ch 7, and repeat.

5. Miss 1 dc, dc in dc around, with 3 dc in 2d of 3 dc at top, miss last dc, ch 5, 2 tc, ch 2 and 2 tc under 1st 2 ch, 2 tc, ch 2, 2 tc, ch 2, 2 tc, ch 2, 2 tc, all under next loop, 2 tc, ch 2, 2 tc, under next loop, ch 5, and repeat.

6. Miss 1 dc, work around point as before, miss last dc, ch 3, 3 tc, 2 ch and 3 tc under each 2 ch of last row, ch 3, and repeat.

7. Miss 3 dc, work around loop as before, miss 3 dc, sh of 3 tc, 2 ch and 3 tc in 1st 2 shs, sh of 8 tc in next, sh of 3 tc, 2 ch and 3 tc in each of next 2, and repeat.

Hexagon Doily.

8. Ch 3, miss 1, fasten in next st; repeat all around.

This border is very effective for table-mats, making the centre of ribbed work, as described in No. 5 Book, either hexagonal or oblong, as liked. For this purpose use No. 25 Barbour's Irish flax thread, Or the border may be added to a linen centre, for doily. Enlarged. the design makes a beautiful cover for a little hexagonal table.

FANCY WORK-BAG.

[Contributed by MERNA LANG, 79 West Street, Hillsdale, Mich.]

Materials: Two spools Barbour's Irish flax thread, No. 35, 3-cord, 200-yards spools, steel hook, size 1, ½ yard silk 19 inches wide, 3 yards ribbon.

Fancy Work-bag.

Ch 5, join.

1. 12 stc in ring.

2. 2 stc in each st of last row.

3. Widen every 5th st, making stc in stc. The bottom of the bag has 25 rows. Widen in 22 rows until you have 180 st; in the last 3 rows do not widen at all.

The leaves are the same as in the "Rose and Leaf Doily," in No. 4, and the centre-piece in No. 6. Ch 14, turn; miss 2, 11 dc in 11 st, 3 in 12th, 10 down other side of ch, turn; ch 1, miss 1 dc, 11 dc in 11 dc, 3 in next, 10 in next 10, turn. Alternate until you have 6 ridges. Join 1st row to bottom of bag by centre st of 3 in last row of leaf; before making last row of next leaf join to 1st leaf with sl-st, work to centre of leaf, miss 11 st of bottom mat, join to next, and finish leaf. In each row are 15 leaves, the 2d and 3d rows being joined to tips of leaves in previous row instead of bottom of bag. The space between leaves is filled with crossed threads, with a wheel woven around them. Finish top of bag with 2½ inch hem and space for draw-strings of the ribbon, pull the crocheted bag on over it, and catch the tip of each leaf in upper row to the silk bag, just below the draw-strings. It is very useful, handsome, and serviceable, as, when soiled, the cover may be removed, laundered, and returned to place.

CHILD'S BONNET.

[Contributed by Miss Estella Ball, Talmage, Kansas.]

Materials: Barbour's Irish flax thread, No. 70, 3-cord, 200-yards spools, either white or ecru, and steel hook, size 00. One spool will be sufficient for the bonnet. If preferred, a coarser number may be chosen.

Wind thread 20 times around a lead-pencil, and work over with 25 dc.

1. Ch 3, tc in back of each st, widening by making 2 tc in 1 st 8 times. Join to top of 3 ch.

2. Ch 3 for a tc, 4 tc in 4 tc, * 2 k-st (for a knot-st draw out loop on needle about ¼ inch long, draw thread through this loop, put needle beween this thread and loop, draw thread through, take up thread and draw through 2 st on hook; repeat for each k-st), 5 tc, the 1st in same place at last, and repeat.

3. 4 tc in 5 tc, leaving last loop on hook each time and drawing thread through all at once, ch 1, 1 k-st, dc in top of 2 k-st of last row, 1 k-st; repeat.

4. 2 k-st, dc in top of 4 tc; repeat.

5. 2 k-st, dc in dc between 2 k-st of last row; repeat.

6. Ch 6, dc in dc between 2 k-st; repeat.

7. Tc in each ch, 2 tc in each dc.

8. Ch 10, * miss 6, dc in next st, turn; ch 3, 5 tc in 5 ch, turn; ch 3, 5 tc in 5 tc, ch 5; repeat. Fasten to 1st 5 st of 10 ch at end of rows, in last block.

9. Ch 8, dc in corner of block; repeat.

10. Like 7th row.

11. Ch 5, miss 3, dc in next st; repeat.

12. Sh of 5 tc in dc between loops of ch, dc in loop, ch 5, dc in next loop; repeat.

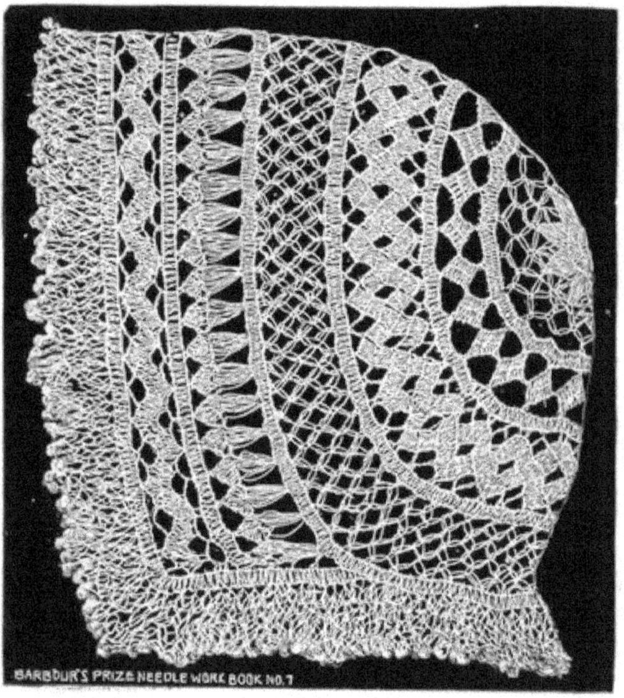

Child's Bonnet.

13. Sh in each ch, 1 dc in each loop and top of sh alternately.

14. Like 12th row, with loop over the sh in 12th row.

15. Like 13th row.

16. Like 12th row.

17. Ch 4, dc in top of sh, ch 4, dc in loop; repeat.

18. Tc in each st.

19. 2 k-st, miss 3, dc in next; repeat.

20, 21, 22. 2 k-st, dc in dc, between k-st of last row.

23. Ch 4, dc in dc; repeat.

24. Tc in each st.

25. Draw thread out ⅝ inch, 5 tc in same place, drawing thread out each time, ch 1, miss 5, 5 tc as before in next st, repeat to within 5 inches of beginning of row, break thread, and fasten in at other end.

26. Sh of 3 tc, 1 ch and 3 tc in 3d of 5 tc (these not drawn out), dc under 1 ch; repeat across; turn.

27. Ch 4, dc under 1 ch; repeat; turn.

28. Tc in each st; turn.

29. Ch 5, miss 4, dc in next; repeat; turn.

30. Like 12th row.

31. Like 13th row.

32. Like 14th row.

33. Like 18th row. Continue the chain along the neck, fastening in ends of previous rows, as convenient, till the row of tc before the drawn-out tc is reached: join to this neatly, turn, make 3 dc in tc, then tc in each st, widening at corners, around to opposite side; work this in the same way; there should be a row of tc entirely around the bonnet.

34, 35, 36, 37. 2 k-st, miss 2, dc in next, and repeat; after the 1st, make dc in dc between k-st of previous row. The last row has a picot edge, thus: 1 k-st, ch 5, dc in dc just made, k-st, dc in dc between k-st of last row, and repeat.

Make ties of ribbon or hemstitched mull, as preferred. A lining may be crocheted of plain tc, or the bonnet lined with any desired fabric. The Irish flax thread is admirable for such articles, as it has a beautiful lustre and launders so well.

INFANT'S BONNET.

[Contributed by Mrs. F. P. BERNARD, Warren, Minn.]

Materials: Barbour's Irish flax thread No. 60, 3-cord, 200-yards spools, and steel hook, size 00. To finish prettily, the bonnet should be lined with China silk, with ties of the same and, if desired, a bow of the silk on top of bonnet. This, however, may be left to the taste of the worker. A spool of thread will be sufficient.

Ch 31.

1. Miss 3, tc in each of 28 st; turn.

2. Ch 5, miss 1 tc, dc in next, repeat across; turn.

3. Ch 5, 2 dc in 5 ch of last row; repeat. Continue like 3d row until there are 21 rows of loops.

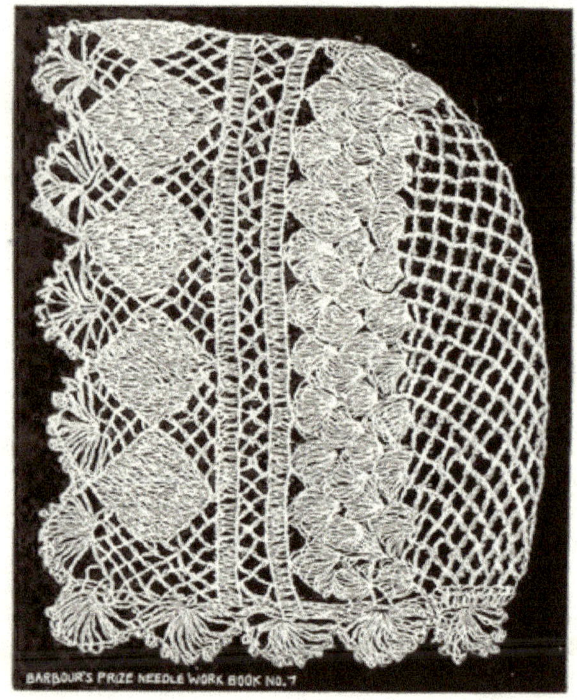

Infant's Bonnet.

22, 23. Draw thread up to centre of last loop, fasten with sc; continue as before.

24, 25. Like 3d row.

26, 27. Like 22d row.

28. Like 3d.

29, 30. Like 22d row. Fasten and cut thread, having finished the crown.

31. Fasten in at base of crown, make 3 tc in side of tc, sh of 5 tc in 2d loop, * fasten with dc in next loop, sh in next, repeat around, finish with 3 tc in tc.

32. 3 tc in 3 tc, ch 3, sc in centre of sh, ch 3, tc in st between shs, repeat from * to end, finishing with 3 tc in 3 tc. This is done in each row, so need not be mentioned.

33. Ch 3 (after the 3 tc), * fasten in centre of sh, sh in tc between shs, repeat from * to end.

34, 35. Shs between shs, each fastened to centre of following sh of last row.

36. Ch 5, sc in centre of sh; repeat.

37. Tc in each st.

38. Ch 6, miss 2 tc, sc in next; repeat.

39. Ch 5, 2 dc in 6 ch, and repeat.

40. Ch 3, sc in centre of 5 ch; repeat.

41. Tc in each st.

42. Ch 5, miss 2, sc in next; repeat.

43. Make 4 loops of 5 ch, fastening in 5 ch of last row, sh of 3 tc between next 2 loops, fasten in centre of next loop, and repeat.

44. Sh each side of sh in last row, with loops between; repeat.

45, 46, 47. Like 44th row, increasing a sh each row, and decreasing a loop.

48, 49, 50, 51. Decrease a sh each row, increasing loops.

52. Loops of 5 ch between loops of last row, fastening every 5th ch to centre of sh.

53. Dtc under 5 ch, ch 4, sc in top of dtc; repeat 9 times for each scallop, working all around.

By using general directions this pattern may be varied as liked. The Irish flax thread has the appearance of silk and does not grow fuzzy or yellow when washed.

TUMBLER OR BONBON DOILY.

[Contributed by Miss ALICE L. BROWN, Putney, Vt.]

Materials: a spool of Barbour's Irish flax thread, No. 100, white, 3-cord, 200-yards spools, crochet hook, size 00, and 4-inch square of linen.

Ch 6, join.

Tumbler or Bonbon Doily.

1. Ch 6, triple tc in loop, * ch 2, triple tc in loop, repeat from * 7 times, making 10 spokes in all, ch 10, sc in 5th st of 10 ch, ch 4, a dc in 1st st of 10 ch, ch 2, triple tc in loop, finish this and 3d wheel the same, turn, and under each 2 ch make a tiny scallop of 1 sc, 2 dc,

1 sc, with 1 sc between wheels; join, and make a close, firm border around space inside of 5 dc on lower spokes, with 2 dc in centre of wheel loop; join and fasten, leaving an end long enough to thread in needle and fill in the centre with 6 crossed threads, and a tiny spider. On your linen mark a circle 3½ inches in diameter, button-hole the edge closely, cut away the outside, and fasten the crocheted points on with needle and thread, or with a sl st when working 3d small scallop. The points may be joined with needle and thread, or when working, with sl st.

A dainty little doily, and easily made. The Irish flax thread gives a richness to the most ordinary work.

LEAF AND STAR CENTRE-PIECE.

[Contributed by CLARA A. STONE, Holliston, Mass.]

Materials: Barbour's Irish flax thread, No. 50, 3-cord, 200-yards spools, and steel hook, size 0. One spool is sufficient.

Ch 12, join.

1. 24 dc in ring, join.

2. Ch 6, miss 2, tc in next, * ch 3, miss 2, tc in next, repeat 6 times, ch 3 and join to 3d of 6 ch.

3. Start each row with 3 ch for a tc, and join to top of 3 ch at end, * 3 tc under 3 ch, ch 2; repeat.

4. 5 tc over 3 tc (making 2 tc in 1st and last), ch 2; repeat.

5, 6, 7, 8, 9, 10, 11, 12, 13. Same as 4th row, increasing 2 tc each time. The 13th row has 23 tc.

14. 21 tc on 23 tc, missing 1st and last, ch 2, tc under 2 ch, ch 2, and repeat.

15. 19 tc on 21 tc, missing 1st and last, ch 3, tc in tc, ch 3; repeat.

16. 17 tc (the diamond decreases regularly), ch 5, tc in tc, ch 5; repeat.

17. 15 tc, ch 4, tc in tc, ch 2, tc in same, ch 2, tc in same, ch 4; repeat.

18. 13 tc, ch 3, 7 tc in last st of 4 ch, ch 2, tc in 2d of 3 tc, ch 2, miss 3, 7 tc in next, ch 3; repeat.

19. 11 tc, ch 4, 7 tc in 7 tc, ch 1, tc in tc, ch 1, 7 tc in 7 tc, ch 4; repeat.

Leaf and Star Centre-piece.

20. 9 tc, ch 6, 5 tc in 7 tc, missing 1st and last, ch 1, 7 tc in top of 1 tc, ch 1, 5 tc in middle 5 of 7 tc, ch 6; repeat.

21. 7 tc, ch 2, miss 2, tc in next, ch 2, miss 2, tc in next, ch 2, 3 tc in 5 tc, ch 2, 7 tc in 7 tc, ch 2, 3 tc in 5 tc, ch 2, miss 2, tc in next, ch 2, miss 2, tc in next, ch 2; repeat.

22. 5 tc, * ch 2, miss 2, tc in next, repeat from * 5 times, 5 tc in 7 tc, missing 1st and last, * ch 2, miss 2, tc in next, repeat 5 times, 4 tc in 4 tc; repeat from 1st *.

23. 3 tc in middle of 5 tc, 7 spaces; repeat all around.

24. Tc in middle of 3 tc, * ch 2, tc under next 2 ch, repeat from * 6 times; repeat from beginning of row.

25, 26, 27. Plain spaces of tc under 2 ch, ch 2, tc under next 2 ch, and repeat.

28. Tc in each st of last row.

29. Tc in 3 st, ch 6, miss 5, dc in each of 7, ch 5; repeat.

30. 5 tc in 3 tc and ch on each side, ch 7, miss 1 dc, 5 dc in 5 dc, ch 7; repeat.

31. 3 tc in ch and 1st 2 tc, ch 4, miss 1 tc, 3 tc in next 3 sts, ch 8, 3 dc in middle of 5 dc, ch 8; repeat.

32. 3 tc in ch and 1st 2 tc, ch 4, tc in 2d st of 4 ch of last row, ch 2, tc in next st, ch 4, miss 2, 3 tc in next 3 st, ch 9, dc in middle of 3 dc, ch 9; repeat.

33. 2 tc on ch and 1 in 1st tc, ch 7, fasten back in 4th st from hook to form a p, ch 2, tc in middle of 4 ch, p, ch 2, tc in 2 ch, ch 6, fasten back in 4th st, ch 1, tc in same place, ch 7, fasten to form p, ch 2, tc in middle of 4 ch, p, ch 2, tc in 3d tc and in 2 st of ch, ch 2; repeat.

If wanted larger, as for an organ-stool tidy, or similar use, coarser linen may be used, or the design may be readily enlarged by making the diamonds wider, repeating the 13th row as many times as necessary. The rows of plain spaces may be increased as well, and any border added that is preferred.

HANDKERCHIEF BORDER.

[Contributed by Mrs. N. E. Rowe, 49 Oak Street, Taunton, Mass.]

Materials: Barbour's Irish flax lace thread, No. 250, 2-cord, 200-yards spools, 6 yards honiton braid, 6-inch square of fine linen lawn, and hook, size 000.

Ch 5, join.

1. Ch 5, * tc in ring, ch 2, repeat from * 6 times, join to 3d of 5 ch.

2. Ch 4, 2 dtc, all under 2 ch of last row, keeping top loop of each on hook and working all off together, ch 5, 3 dtc under same

ch, working off as before, make 2 groups of 3 dtc, separated by 5 ch under each 2 ch, and join last 5 ch with sc to top of 1st 4 ch.

3. Cut 8 medallions, and join ends. Sc up to 3d of 5 ch, * ch 3, sc in 1st third of medallion, ch 3, sc in next 5 ch, ch 3, fasten in medallion about 3/16 inch from 1st fastening, ch 3, sc in next 5 ch,

Handkerchief Border.

and repeat from * all around, completing a wheel. To join, fasten thread in 1st loop of medallion in the wheel taken for the 1st one, ch 7, sc in centre of medallion, ch 7, sc in last loop of same, ch 7, sc in 1st loop of next medallion, ch 20, sc in centre, ch 20, sc in last loop, ch 7, sc in 1st loop of next medallion, and repeat, filling 3 medallions with short and 2 with long chs. For the 2d wheel, fasten thread as before, ch 3, sc in 4th st of 7 ch (of 1st wheel, in front of the long ch), ch 3, sc in 1st loop of next medallion, ch 3, sc in 4th st of 7 ch, ch 3, sc in centre of same medallion, ch 3, sc in 4th of 7 ch, ch 3, sc in last loop of medallion, ch 3, sc in 4th st of 7 ch, ch 3, sc in 1st loop of next medallion, ch 20, sc in centre of same, ch 20, sc in last loop of same, ch 7, sc in 1st loop of next; repeat, working 4 medallions with short and 4 with long chs. This completes 2d wheel; join 5 more like last, making 7 in a strip.

To join the corner wheel, fasten thread in 1st loop of medallion, ch 3, sc in 4th st of 7 ch of 1st wheel, ch 3, sc in centre of same medallion, ch 3, sc in 4th st of next 7 ch, ch 3, sc in last loop of medallion, ch 3, sc in 4th st of next 7 ch, ch 3, 1 sc in 1st loop of next medallion, ch 20, sc in centre of same medallion, ch 20, sc in last loop of medallion, ch 7, sc in 1st loop of next, ch 7, sc in centre of same, ch 7, sc in last loop. Fourth wheel, to be joined to the corner one: Fasten thread in 1st loop of medallion, ch 3, sc in 4th st of 7 ch of corner wheel, ch 3, sc in centre of same medallion, ch 3, sc in 4th st of 7 ch, ch 3, sc in last loop, ch 3, sc in 4th st of 7 ch, ch 3, sc in 1st loop of next medallion, ch 20, sc in centre, ch 10, put needle through loops of each 20 ch, make 1 sc, ch 10, sc in last loop of medallion, ch 3, sc in 4th st of next 7 ch (of 2d wheel), ch 3, sc in 1st loop of next medallion, ch 3, sc in 4th st of next 7 ch, ch 3, sc in centre, ch 3, sc in 4th st of next 7 ch, ch 3, sc in last loop of medallion, ch 3, sc in 4th st of next 7 ch, ch 3, sc in 1st loop of next medallion, ch 20, sc in centre of same, ch 20, sc in last loop of same, ch 7, sc in 1st loop of medallion, ch 7, sc in centre, ch 7, sc in last. The other corners are joined in same manner.

After all the wheels are made and joined, work around the centre as follows: Fasten thread in last 7 ch next to corner, ch 10, put needle through each loop of 20 ch, fasten with sc, ch 10, sc in next 7 ch (of next wheel), ch 3, sc in next 7 ch, ch 3, sc in next 7 ch, ch 3, sc in next 7 ch, ch 10, join the loops of 20 ch as before, and repeat around centre. For the picot edge, fasten thread in 1st loop of medallion, ch 9, sc in 3d st of 9 ch to form a p, ch 3, sc in centre of same medallion, ch 9, sc in 3d st, ch 3, sc in last loop, ch 9, sc in 3d st, ch 3, sc in 1st loop of next medallion, and repeat.

These wheels, joined, make beautiful tidies, cushion-covers, border for ties, etc., or in coarser thread, with novelty braid, form a handsome finish for table-covers, bureau-scarfs, and similar articles.

DOILY WITH MALTESE BRAID.

[Contributed by Mrs. R. A. HAWKINS, Okolona, Miss.]

Doily with Maltese Braid.

Materials: Barbour's Irish flax thread, No. 120, 3-cord, 200-yards spools, steel hook, size 000, square of linen 4 × 4 inches, and ½-inch pin or staple.

Directions are given for Maltese work in Nos. 4, 5, and 6 of Barbour's Prize Needlework Series. This is slightly heavier. Make a loop in thread, and place it on the prong, holding this down so the work will slip off readily. Turn pin over, make 2 dc on thread, * turn, dc in 1st dc and 1 dc in centre, 1 dc under loop, turn. This makes 3 dc between loops. Repeat to required length. Make a ch on both sides of braid, catching 1 loop in every 2d ch. Baste braid to pattern, following instructions given for Battenburg lace-making in Book No. 6. For the rings, take Barbour's flossette, size ***, wind 12 times around small pencil, and buttonhole with the No. 102 thread, finishing each with 11 p in point de Venise. Fasten rings in place by carrying thread back and forth from braid to p, fastening thread each time with a knot-stitch so it will not slip. When lace is complete, baste centre to inner circle of braid, remove from pattern, baste on right side up, and buttonhole around centre with flossette. Finish outer edge with loops of 3 ch, caught in each p.

The Maltese braid may be used for any Battenburg pattern instead of the plain braid. The effect is very lovely.

ENGLISH POINT, LEAF LACE.

[Contributed by S. VILETTA DOANE, Essex, Conn.]

Materials: Barbour's Irish flax thread, No. 100, 3-cord, 200-yards spools; 2 spools for 1 yard of lace; and 2 steel needles, No. 18.

Cast on, very loosely, 52 sts.

1. F, k 6, o, n, o, k 5, (o, k 1, o, n, k 1, n,) o, k 1, o, k 5, o, k 1 o, k 1, (o, k 2, n, o, k 1,) o 2, k 1, o, n, o, k 3, n, n, k 3, o, n, k 3.

2. K 5, p 13, (o, k 3, o, n 3 tog,) o, p 4, o, p 7, o, k 2, (o, n 3 tog, o, k 3,) o, p 14, f, loop on loosely 5 new sts.

3. O, k 5, o, n, o, k 7, o, k 1, o, k 6, (o, n, k 1, n, o, k 1,) o, n, k 2, o, k 8, o, n, o, k 3, (o, k 1, o, n, k 1, n,) o, k 3, o, n, o, k 2, n, n, k 2, o, n, k 3.

4. K 5, p 13, (k 3 tog, o, k 3, o,) p 15, o, k 3 tog, (o, k 3, o, k 3 tog,) o, p 26.

5. O, k 7, o, k 1, o, k 9, o, k 1, o, k 9, (o, k 1, o, n, k 2,) o, k 3, o, k 1, o, k 10, o, k 5, (o, k 2, n, o, k 1,) o 2, k 5, o, n, o, k 1, n, n, k 1, o, n, k 3.

6. K 5, p 13, (o, k 3, o, n 3 tog,) o, p 24, (o, n 3 tog, o, k 3,) o, p 32.

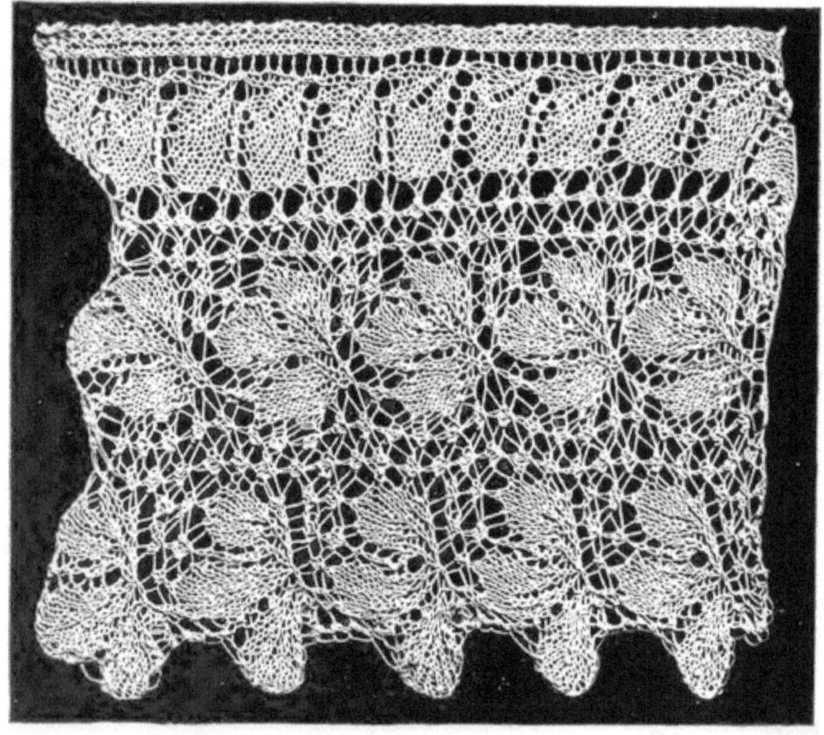

English Point, Leaf Lace.

7. O, k 9, o, n, k 2, n, n, k 3, o, n, o, k 3, n, n, k 3, (o, n, k 1, n, o, k 1,) o, k 5, o, n, o, k 2, n 4 times, k 1, o, k 8, (o, k 1, o, n, k 1, n,) o, k 7, o, n, o, n, n, o, n, k 3.

8. K 5, p 13, (n 3 tog, o, k 3, o,) p 24, (o, k 3, o, k 3 tog,) o, p 31

9. O, n, k 2, n, n, k 3, o, k 2, n, n, k 1, n, o, n, k 1, n 3 tog, n 3 tog, k 1, n, (o, k 1, o, n, k 1, n,) o, k 7, o, n 4 times, o, k 2, n, n, k 3, (o, n, k 1, n, o, k 1,) o, k 9, o, n, o, n, o, n, k 3.

10. K 5, p 13, (o, k 3, o, n 3 tog,) p 22, (o, n 3 tog, o, k 3,) o 2, p 23.

11. O, n, k 1, n, n, k 2, o, n 4 times, o, n 3 times, o, k 1, (o, n, k 1, n, o, k 1,) o, k 9, o, n 6 times, k 1, o, k 1, (o, k 1, o, n, k 1, n,) o, k 1, o, n, o, k 3, n, n, k 3, o, n, k 3.

12. K 5, p 13, (n 3 tog, o, k 3, o,) k 1, o, p 18, (o, k 3, o, n 3 tog,) o, k 3, o, p 16.

13. O, n 8 times, o, k 1, o, k 2, n, (o, k 1, o, n, k 1, n,) o, n, k 2, n, n, k 2, n 4 times, k 1, o, k 1, (o, n, k 1, n, o, k 1,) o 2, k 3, o, n, o, k 2, n, n, k 2, o, n, k 3.

14. K 5, p 13, (o, k 3, o, n 3 tog,) o, k 3, o, p 13, (n 3 tog, o, k 3, o) 2 times, p 9.

15. O, k 1, n, n, n 4 tog, (o, n, k 1, n, o, k 1) 2 times, o, n 6 times, (o, k 1, o, n, k 1, n) 2 times, o, k 5, o, n, o, k 1, n, n, k 1, o, n, k 3.

16. K 5, p 13, (n 3 tog, o, k 3, o) 2 times, p 6, (o, k 3, o, n 3 tog) 2 times, o, k 1, o, p 5, pick up 2 loops on the side of the edge leaf, and f them together.

17. F, n, n 3 tog, o, k 3, (o, k 1, o, n, k 1, n) 2 times, n, n, n, (n, k 1, n, o, k 1, o) 2 times, o, k 7, o, n, o, n, n, o, n, k 3.

18. K 5, p 13, (o, k 3, o, n 3 tog) 5 times, o, n, k 1, f.

19. F, k 1, n, (o, k 1, o, n, k 1, n) 5 times, k 9, o, n, o, n, o, n, k 3.

20. K 5, p 13, (n 3 tog, o, k 3, o) 5 times, k 2, f.

Repeat from row 1st.

To f (or fagot) o 2, p 2 tog. This o 2 makes but 1 st when knitting back. In making an over or o be sure to put the thread over or around the needle in such a manner that it can easily be knitted for 1 st when knitting back. O 2 should be knitted as 2 sts when knitting back, except in fagots. Care should be taken not to knit too tight, as it causes the lace to draw. The lace may be made of any desired width by repeating the parts in parenthesis the requisite number of times, allowing 6 sts for each repeat. A handsome narrow edge may be knit by using in the odd-numbered rows the directions from the first through the first parentheses, and adding 3 plain sts for heading, and in the even rows directions for the last parentheses, and from thence to the end of the row. A separate insertion is formed by directions in *both* parentheses, *with* the directions between, and 3 plain sts added to *each* edge.

CORSET-COVER YOKE.

[Contributed by Mrs. CARRIE FISHER, Wilmington, Vt.]

Materials: Barbour's Irish flax thread, No. 120, 3-cord, 200-yards spools, 2 No. 19 needles, or finer if desired.

Cast on 43 sts, k across plain.

1. O, n, k 1, f (that is, o 2, p 2 tog), n, o 2, n, f, k 8, n, o, k 1, o, n, k 8, f, n, o 2, n, f, k 3.
2. O, n, k 1, f, k 2, p 1, k 1, f, p 21, f, k 2, p 1, k 1, f, k 3.
3. O, n, k 1, f, k 4, f, k 7, n, o, k 3, o, n, k 7, f, k 4, f, k 3.
4. O, n, k 1, f, k 4, f, p 21, f, k 4, f, k 3.
5. O, n, k 1, f, n, o 2, n, f, k 7, n, o, k 3, o, n, k 7, f, n, o 2, n, f, k 3.
6. Like 2d row.
7. O, n, k 1, f, k 4, f, k 9, o, k 3 tog, o, k 9, f, k 4, f, k 3.
8. Like 4th row.
9. O, n, k 1, f, n, o 2, n, f, k 2, n, o, k 1, o, n, k 7, n, o, k 1, o, n, k 2, f, n, o 2, n, f, k 3.
10. Like 2d row.
11. O, n, k 1, f, k 4, f, k 1, n, o, k 3, o, n, k 5, n, o, k 3, o, n, k 1, f, k 4, f, k 3.
12. Like 4th row.
13. O, n, k 1, f, n, o 2, n, f, k 1, n, o, k 3, o, n, k 5, n, o, k 3, o, n, k 1, f, n, o 2, n, f, k 3.
14. Like 2d row.

15. O, n, k 1, f, k 4, f, k 3, o, k 2 tog, o, k 9, o, k 3 tog, o, k 3, f, k 4, f, k 3.

16. Like 4th row.

Corset-cover Yoke.

Repeat from 1st row for length desired. Any pretty knitted edge may be added to the insertion, making a handsome pattern for wide lace. For the narrow neck-strip, cast on 13 sts, k across plain.

1. Sl 1, k 1, f, n, o 2, n, f, k 3.

2. O, n, k 1, f, k 2, p 1, k 1, f, k 2.

3. Sl 1, k 1, f, k 4, f, k 3.

4. O, n, k 1, f, k 4, f, k 2.

Repeat for length required. Join to wide insertion, drawing narrow ribbon through eyelets, as shown.

ROSE-LEAF AND FERN LACE.

[Contributed by Miss S. VILETTA DOANE, Essex, Conn.]

Materials: Barbour's Irish flax thread, No. 80, 3-cord, 200-yards spools, and 2 steel needles, No. 18.

Cast on 19 sts.

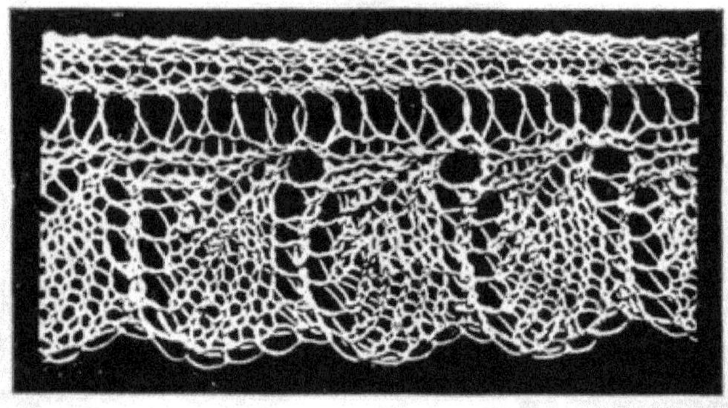

Rose-Leaf and Fern Lace.

1. O, k 1, o, n, o, k 3, n, n, k 2, n, o, n, k 3.

2, 4, 6, 8. K 5, p 13.

3. O, k 3, o, n, o, k 2, n, n, k 2, o, n, k 3.

5. O, k 5, o, n, o, k 1, n, n, k 1, o, n, k 3.

7. O, k 7, o, n, o, n, n, o, n, k 3.

9. O, k 9, o, n, o, n, o, n, k 3.

10. K 5, p 14.

Repeat from 1st row.

TATTED DOILY.

[Contributed by Mrs. P. M. Hobson, Rutherford, N.J.]

Materials: Barbour's Irish flax thread, No. 150, 3-cord, 200-yards spools, and tatting shuttle.

Tatted Doily.

The centre of the rosette is formed of 12 p, with 2½ dk between each, close and tie. The small ring is of 3 p, with 2 dk between each, joining middle p to centre already made. * Turn over, make a ring of 7 p with 2 dk between each; turn, make 2 dk, join to p on small ring, 2 dk, join to centre, 2 dk, p, 2 dk, close; repeat until you have the rosette of 12 rings, alternating small and large; tie. Join 4 rosettes diamond-shape. For the bars, begin with a small ring, turn, make a large ring, join to diamond between middle p of ring, repeat once, make 2 large and 3 small rings, join to next rosette of diamond. When making the ends of bars, the 2 small rings and 1 large ring in the centre are made without turning work.

This doily suggests a very pretty tidy, made of No. 60 or No. 70 Irish flax thread. If liked, the diamonds may be made of 9 rosettes, 3 each way, or 16, 4 each way, with ribbon run between them, if preferred, instead of using the tatted bars. These rosettes make a lovely edge for linen doilies or centre-pieces.

CHILD'S TATTED YOKE.

[Contributed by MRS. MARY KNIGHT, Minneota, Minn.]

Materials: Barbour's Irish flax thread, No. 60, in balls, or 3-cord, 200-yards spools, with tatting shuttles.

Make the wheels as follows, beginning at lower edge of front: A ring of 8 p, each separated by 2 dk, close; 2 dk, p, 2 dk, join to a p of ring, 2 dk, p, 2 dk, close; join 2d thread, 4 dk, 5 p, each separated by 2 dk, 4 dk; with 1 thread, make another small ring, and alternate until there are eight of each, the small rings joined to the middle ring. This completes the wheel. Cut a paper pattern of the size of yoke required. That shown has 10 wheels for lower row of front, each joined to the preceding by middle picots of 2 scallops. The sample clearly shows how the yoke is formed. Fill edges at neck and back with half wheels, and crochet a ch around, if desired.

In these days of laces, tatting is again in high favor. It may be as delicate as desired. The little wheels described may be used for a blouse, permitting the showing through of a silk lining. Simply have a pattern, well-fitted over the shoulders as a guide — an old dress-waist, with the under-arm seams and darts ripped serves well.

Join the wheels to cover the pattern, and remove when completed. Crocheted wheels may be used, if liked, and a combination of ecru

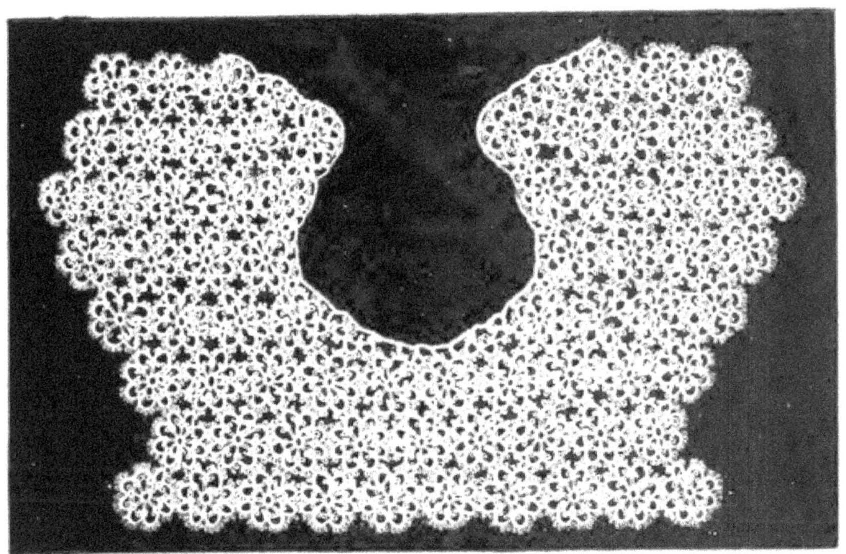

Child's Tatted Yoke.

and white flax thread is very effective. Or a gray over scarlet or cardinal lining may be used. With these blouses a silk waist that is a little "gone by" may be used, forming a really elegant toilet.

NETTED DOILIES.

[Contributed by CLARA F. ATWOOD, 126 Princeton Street, East Boston, Mass.]

Materials: Barbour's Irish flax thread, No. 120, 3-cord, 200-yards spools, small netting needle (No. 19), mesh-sticks, ¼ and ⅓ inch wide, knitting-needles No. 12 and No. 14.

Doily No. 1.—36 sts in loop over ¼-in. mesh; 3 rounds over needle; 2 sts in 1, over mesh; 4 rounds over needle, 1 round over mesh; 1 round over needle, draw left st through right, net, then net right st through left, making a twisted st; 2 rounds over needle; 1 over mesh; 1 over mesh, netting 3 sts into 2 sts taken together; 3 over needle; 1 round, netting 2 sts in 1, over mesh; 3 over needle; 1 over mesh; 11 over needle, making a cross-st by netting first the

Netted Doilies.

left, then the right st; 2 over needle; 1 over mesh, with doubled thread.

Doily No. 2. — 34 sts in loop, over mesh; 3 rounds over needle;

1 round, netting 2 sts in 1, over mesh: 4 over needle; 1 over mesh; 1 over needle, twisted-st, as above; 2 over needle; 1 over mesh; 1 over mesh, netting 3 sts in 2 taken together; 3 over needle; 1 over mesh; 1 over mesh, 2 sts taken together, with doubled thread; 1 over mesh, into each st with doubled thread; 1 over mesh, single thread, putting 3 sts in 1; 3 over needle; 1 over mesh, netting 7 sts into every 5th; 1 over needle, netting end st through middle st in the space, forming a sh; 1 over needle.

Doily No. 3. — 36 sts in loop, over ⅓-in. mesh; 5 rounds over needle; 1 over mesh, 3 sts in 1; 5 over needle; 1 over mesh, doubled thread; 1 over needle, netting first left, then right, making the cross-st; 2 over needle; 1 over mesh, 2 sts in 1; 1 over needle, 2 sts together; 1 over needle; 4 over needle twice, then over needle once, in every other st, making picot edge; 1 over mesh; 1 over mesh, 8 sts in every other st; 1 over needle, drawing loop through extra loop, for sh border; 1 over needle.

Doily No. 4. — 32 sts in loop, over ¼-in. mesh; 4 rounds over needle; 1 over mesh, 2 sts in 1; 4 over needle; 1 over mesh; 1 over needle, making the twisted st; 3 over needle; 1 over mesh, netting 1, then 2 sts in 1, alternately; 3 over needle; 1 over mesh, with doubled thread; 1 over needle, making the cross-st; 1 over needle; 1 over mesh, netting into every 2d st; 1 over mesh, netting 1 st and 7 sts alternately, for pineapple edge; 1 over needle, 6 sts into 7 sts, thread over needle 3 times between; 1 over needle, 5 sts in 6, thread over 4 times, and so continue to end of point, decreasing sts, and increasing the overs.

Doily No. 5. — 38 sts over mesh, in loop; 4 rounds over needle; 1 over mesh, 2 sts in 1; 4 over needle; 1 over mesh; 1 over needle, making the twist-st; 1 over needle; 1 over mesh; 1 over mesh, 3 sts into 2 taken together; 3 over needle; 1 over mesh, 2 sts in 1; 2 over needle; 1 over needle, netting 9 sts, thread over twice, leaving 1 st; net 9, and so on; 1 over needle, netting 8 sts in 9 sts, thread over 3 times, etc.; 1 over needle, netting 7 sts in 8 sts, thread over 4 times, and continue to end of point.

Doily No. 6. — 37 sts in loop, over mesh; 4 rounds over No. 12 needle; 1 over mesh, 2 sts in 1; 7 over needle No. 14; 1 over mesh;

twist 1, then 2 sts in 1, alternately; 4 over needle; 1 over mesh; 1 over mesh, 3 sts in 2, taken together; 2 over needle No. 14; 1 over needle No. 14, netting 7 sts, thread over twice, miss 1 st, and repeat; 1 over same needle, net 6 sts, thread over 3 times; 1 over needle, netting 5 sts, thread over 4 times; continue to end of point.

When size is not mentioned, the ¼-in. mesh is used, and No. 14 needle. Although but four doilies are illustrated, directions are given for the set of six. Nothing daintier for a little tea-table can be imagined. Instructions for netting are very accurately given, with complete illustrations, in No. 5 of Barbour's Prize Needlework Series.

BOBBIN LACES.

[Contributed by Miss EDNA D. STODDARD, Roxbury, Mass.]

Lace, No. 1. Materials: Barbour's Irish flax thread, No. 80, 3-cord, 200-yards spools, 14 pairs of bobbins. Pin 6 pairs in 35, 3 pairs in 31, 3 pairs in 34, and 2 pairs in 33.

Ctc 8th and 9th, pin in 1; ctc to left, using 6th pair, pin in 2; ctc to right using 10th, pin in 3; to left, using 7th, pin in 4; to right, using 12th, pin in 5; to left, using 8th, pin in 6; to right, using 10th. (a) Wt 11th and 12th, ctc 11th, 12th, 13th, and 14th, using a pair as single bobbin, wt 11th

and 12th, 13th and 14th; make a picot, putting pin under thread of last bobbin from right to left, back over from left to right, forming a loop, then put pin in 7; 2 wt 13th and 14th, picot, pin in 8; 2 wt as before, picot, pin in 9; close with wt, ctc with 11th to 14th as before, using pairs as single bobbins, wt 13th, 14th, and 11th and 12th (a), ctc 10th and 11th, 11th and 12th, pin in 10, ctc to left, using 8th. Tw 6th, ctc 5th and 6th, pin in 11, close with ctc; tw 5th, (b) ctc 4th and 5th, 3d and 4th, tw 3d once, wt 2d and 3d, 1st and 2d, pin in 12; wt 1st and 2d to close, wt 2d and 3d, ctc 3d and 4th, 4th and 5th (b). Tw 5th, 6th, 7th, and 8th 3 times, (c) ctc 6th and 7th, 7th and 8th, 5th and 6th, 6th and 7th, pin in 13; ctc 6th and 7th (to close) 7th, and 8th, 5th and 6th, 6th and 7th (c), tw all 3 times. Repeat (b) to (b), pin in 14; tw 5th once, ctc 5th and 6th, pin in 15; close with ctc, tw 5th once, repeat from (b) to (b), pin in 16; tw 5th and 6th once, ctc 8th and 9th, 9th and 10th: repeat (a) to (a), putting pins, respectively, in 17, 18, 19. Ctc 10th and 11th, 11th and 12th, pin in 20; ctc to left, using 8th, pin in 21; to right, using 10th; repeat from (a) to (a), putting pins in 22, 23, and 24; ctc 10th and 11th, 11th and 12th, pin in 25; to left, using 7th, pin in 26; to right, using 10th, pin in 27; to left, using 6th, pin in 28; to right, using 9th, pin in 29; to left, using 5th, pin in 30; to right, using 8th, pin in 31; to left, using 6th; tw 5th once, repeat from (b) to (b), putting pin in 32; tw 5th once, ctc 5th and 6th, pin in 33; ctc to right, using 8th, tw 5th once, repeat from (b) to (b), pin in 34; tw 5th once; tw 9th and 10th, 3 times, wt 11th and 12th, ctc with 11th, 12th, 13th, and 14th, as single bobbins, 2 wt 13th and 14th, wt 11th and 12th; repeat (c) to (c), using 9th, 10th, 11th, and 12th pairs, putting pin in 35. Tw 9th and 10th 3 times, wt 11th, and 12th, ctc with 11th, 12th, 13th, and 14th, as single bobbins; wt 11th and 12th, 13th and 14th. Repeat from beginning.

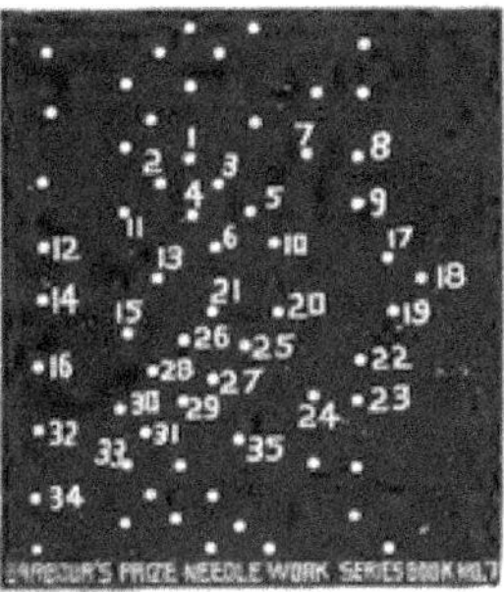

Insertion No. 2. Materials: Barbour's Irish flax thread, No. 150, 3-cord, 200-yards spools, and 16 pairs of bobbins. Pin 2 pairs in 7, 23, 36, 37, 38, 27, and 13, 1 pair in 34 and 35.

Left edge: Wt 1st and 2d pairs, pin in 1; * close with wt; tw 1st and 2d pairs once; ctc 2d and 3d, 3d and 4th *, pin in 2, close with ctc; * ctc to left, using 2d; tw 2d twice, wt 1st and 2d, pin in 3; do not close, *; repeat from 1st to 2d *, ctc with 4th and 5th, pin in 4, repeat

from 3d to 4th *, pin in 5; repeat from 1st to 2d * pin in 6; repeat from 3d to 4th *, pin in 7, repeat from 1st to 2d *.

Right edge: Wt 15th and 16th, pin in 8, * close with wt, tw both pairs once. Ctc 14th and 15th, 13th and 14th *, pin in 9, close with ctc; * ctc to right, using 15th, tw 15th twice, wt 15th and 16th, pin in 10, do not close, *; repeat from 1st to 2d *; ctc 12th and 13th, pin in 11, close with ctc; repeat from 3d to 4th *, putting pin in 12. Repeat from 1st to 2d *, pin in 13; repeat from 3d to 4th *, pin in 14; repeat from 1st to 2d *.

Centre: Wt 8th and 9th, pin in 15, close with ctc; ctc 9th and 10th, 10th and 11th, pin in 16; ctc to left, using 6th, pin in 17; to right, using 12th, pin in 18; to left, using 5th, pin in 19; to right, using 9th, pin in 20; to left, using 5th, pin in 21; to right, using 8th, pin in 22; to left, using 5th, tw 5th twice, ctc 4th and 5th, pin in 23; close (as usual) with ctc, tw 5th twice, ctc with 5th and 6th, pin in 24; ctc to right, using 7th. Commencing with 9th and 10th, ctc to right, using 12th, pin in 25; to left, using 9th, pin in 26; to right, using 12th, tw 12th twice, ctc 12th and 13th, pin in 27, close with ctc, tw 12th twice, ctc 11th and 12th, pin in 28; ctc to left, using 10th, tw 8th and 9th twice, wt 8th and 9th, tw once; ctc 9th and 10th, pin in 29; to right, using 12th, pin in 30; to left, using 9th; ctc 7th and 8th, pin in 31; ctc to left, using 5th, pin in 32; to right, using 9th, pin in 33; again, to right, using 12th, pin in 34; to left, using 5th, pin in 35; ctc to right, using 11th, pin in 36; to left, using 6th, pin in 37; to right, using 9th, pin in 38, close with ctc; ht 8th and 9th; wt 10th and 11th, tw 12th twice; wt 6th and 7th, tw 5th twice; ctc 13th and 14th, 14th and 15th, tw 15th twice, ctc 3d and 4th, 2d and 3d, tw 2d twice.

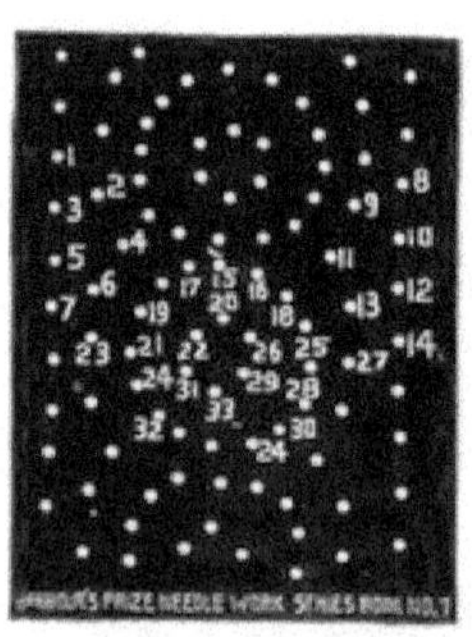

DIAMOND LACE.

Materials: Barbour's new Irish flax lace thread, No. 250, 3-cord, 200-yards spools, 31 pairs of bobbins, and lace-desk, or suitable cushion. Pin 4 pairs in 150, 3 in 149, 1 in 139, 127, 121, 117, 110, 106, 99, 90, 91, 92, 93, 94, 2 in 95, 1 in 82, 81, 80, 79, 78, 151, 152, and 3 in 153.

Ht 5th and 6th, pin in 1; ht 6th and 7th, pin in 2; ht to left, using 4th, pin in 3; to right, using 8th, pin in 4; to left, using 3d, pin in 5; to right, using 9th, pin in 6; to left, using 4th, pin in 7; to right, using 10th, pin in 8; to left, using 4th; (a) wt 2d and 3d, 1st and 2d, pin in 9, wt to close, wt 2d and 3d (a); ht 3d and 4th, pin in 10; ht to right, using 11th, pin in 11; to left, using 4th, pin in 12; to right, using 10th, pin in 13; to left, using 4th; repeat (a) to (a), putting pin in 14; ht 3d and 4th, in pin 15; to right, using 9th, pin in 16; to left, using 4th, pin in 17; ht to right, using 8th, pin in 18; ht to left, using 4th, repeat (a) to (a), putting pin in 19; ht 3d and 4th, pin in 20; to right, using 7th, pin in 21; to left, using 4th, pin in 22; to right, using 6th, pin in 23; repeat (a) to (a), pin in 24; ht 3d and 4th, pin in 25; repeat (a) to (a), pin in 26; ht 4th and 5th, pin in 27; ht 3d and 4th, pin in 28; repeat (a) to (a), putting pin in 29.

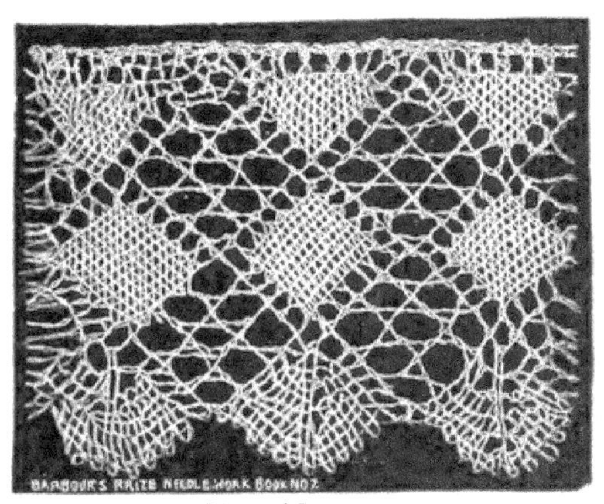

Diamond Lace.

Ht 17th and 18th, pin in 30; ht to right, using 19th, pin in 31; to left, using 16th, pin in 32; to right, using 20th, pin in 33; to left, using 15th, pin in 34; to right, using 21st, pin in 35; to left, using 14th, pin in 36; to right, using 22d, pin in 37; to left, using 13th, pin in 38; to right, using 23d, pin in 39; to left, using 12th, pin in 40; to right, using 22d, pin in 41; to left, using 13th, pin in 42; to right, using 21st, pin in 43; to left, using 14th, pin in 44; to right, using 20th, pin in 45; to left, using 15th, pin in 46; to right, using 19th, pin in 47; to left, using 16th, pin in 48; to right, using 18th, pin in 49.

To form open ground, ht 11th and 12th, pin in 50; close with ht, then twist each pair once. Remember to make this twist after each closing, as it will not again be mentioned. Ht 12th and 13th, pin in 51; 13th and 14th, pin in 52; 14th and 15th, pin in 53; 15th and 16th, pin in 54; 16th and 17th, pin in 55; ht 10th and 11th, pin in 56; 12th and 13th, pin in 57; 14th and 15th, pin in 58; 9th and 10th, pin in 59; 10th and 11th, pin in 60; 11th and 12th, pin in 61; 12th and 13th, pin in 62; 13th and 14th, pin in 63; 14th and 15th, pin in 64; 8th and 9th, pin in 65; 10th and 11th, pin in 66; 12th and 13th, pin in 67; 7th and 8th, pin in 68; 8th and 9th, pin in 69; 9th and 10th, pin in 70; 10th and 11th, pin in 71; 11th and 12th, pin in 72; 12th and 13th, pin in 73; 6th and 7th, pin in 74; 8th and 9th, pin in 75; 10th and 11th, pin in 76; 5th and 6th, pin in 77; 6th and 7th, pin in 78; 7th and 8th, pin in 79; 8th and 9th, pin in 80; 9th and 10th, pin in 81; 10th and 11th, pin in 82; ht 23d and 24th, pin in 83; 22d and 23d, pin in 84; 21st and 22d, pin in 85; 20th and 21st, pin in 86; 19th and 20th, pin in 87; 18th and 19th, pin in 88; continue down the diagonal in same way to pin in 95, between 11th and 12th pairs. Ht 24th and 25th, pin in 96; 22d and 23d, pin in 97; 20th and 21st, pin in 98; 18th and 19th, pin in 99; 25th and 26th, pin in 100; 24th and 25th, pin in 101; work down the diagonal thus to 106, between 19th and 20th pairs; ht 26th and 27th, pin in 107; 24th and 25th, pin in 108; 22d and 23d, pin in 109; 20th and 21st, pin in 110; 27th and

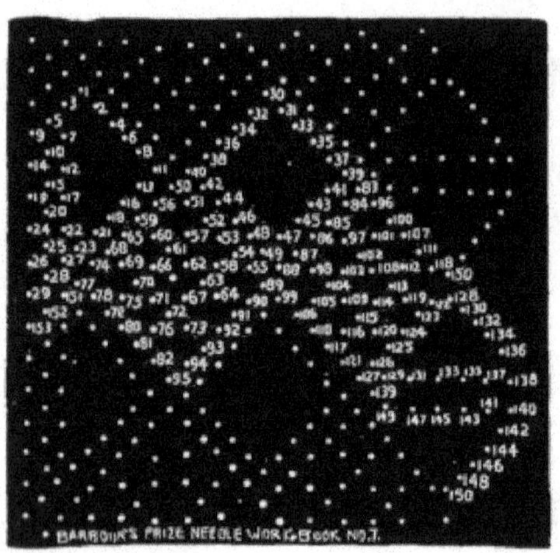

28th, pin in 111; 26th and 27th, pin in 112; work down diagonal to 117, between 21st and 22d pairs; ht 28th and 29th, pin in 118; 26th and 27th, pin in 119; 24th and 25th, pin in 120; 22d and 23d, pin in 121; wt 29th and 30th; ht 28th and 29th, pin in 122; 27th and 28th, pin in 123; work down diagonal to 127, between 23d and 24th pairs. This completes the open grounds, and the pairs are not to be twisted after closing in following directions:

Wt 30th and 31st, pin in 128; wt to left, using 25th pair, pin in 129; (b) wt to right, using 31st pair, pin in 130 (b); wt to left, using 26th, pin in 131; repeat (b) to (b), putting pin in 132; to left, using 27th, pin in 133; repeat (b) to (b), pin in 134; to left, using 28th, pin in 135; repeat (b) to (b), pin in 136; to left, using 29th, pin in 137; repeat (b) to (b), pin in 138; to left, using 24th, pin in 139; repeat (b) to (b), pin in 140; to left, using 29th, pin in 141; (b) to (b), pin in 142; to left, using 28th, pin in 143; (b) to (b), pin in 144; to left, using 27th, pin in 145; (b) to (b), pin in 146; to left, using 26th, pin in 147; (b) to (b), pin in 148; to left, using 25th, pin in 149; (b) to (b), pin in 150.

This completes the scallop. Ht 4th and 5th, pin in 151; ht 3d and 4th, pin in 152; repeat (a) to (a), pin in 153.

This finishes the pattern of lace. The insertion is made in the same way, omitting the scallop and working the edge according to directions given.

EDGING.

Materials: Barbour's new Irish flax lace thread, No. 250, 12 pairs bobbins. Pin 3 pairs in 23 and in 27, 6 pairs in 28.

Open hole ground: Ht 3d and 4th (pairs), pin in 1; ht 4th and 5th, pin in 2; ht 5th and 6th, pin in 3; wt 2d and 3d, 1st and 2d, pin in 4; wt 2d and 3d; ht 3d and 4th, pin in 5; ht 4th and 5th, pin in 6; wt 2d and 3d, 1st and 2d, pin in 7; wt 2d and 3d; ht 3d and 4th, pin in 8; wt 2d and 3d, 1st and 2d, pin in 9; wt 2d and 3d.

Scallop: Ctc 9th and 10th, pin in 10; (a) ctc to right, using 11th pair, tw 11th twice, wt 11th and 12th, pin in 11; tw 11th once (a), ctc to left, using 8th pair, pin in 12; repeat (a) to (a), pin in 13; ctc to left, using 7th, pin in 14; repeat (a) to (a), pin in 15; ctc to left, using 6th pair, pin in 16; repeat (a) to (a), pin in 17; ctc to left, using 7th, pin in 18; repeat (a) to (a), pin in 19; ctc to left, using 8th, pin in 20; repeat (a) to (a), pin in 21; ctc to left, using 9th pair, pin in 22; repeat (a) to (a), pin in 23; etc 10th and 11th.

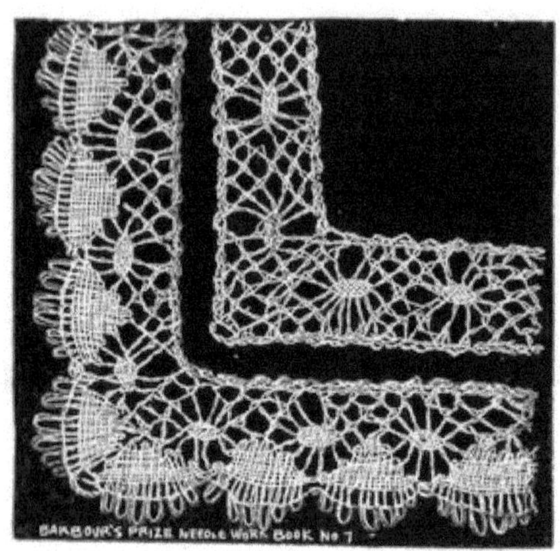

Open hole ground: Tw 6th once, ht 5th and 6th, pin in 24; ht 4th and 5th, pin in 25; ht 3d and 4th, pin in 26; wt 2d and 3d, 1st and 2d, pin in 27; wt 2d and 3d.

Spider: Tw 4th, 5th, and 6th twice, 7th, 8th, and 9th 3 times; (b) ctc 6th and 7th, 7th and 8th, 8th and 9th, 5th and 6th, 6th and 7th, 7th and 8th, 4th and 5th, 5th and 6th, 6th and 7th (b), pin in 28; repeat (b) to (b), twist all pairs used 3 times.

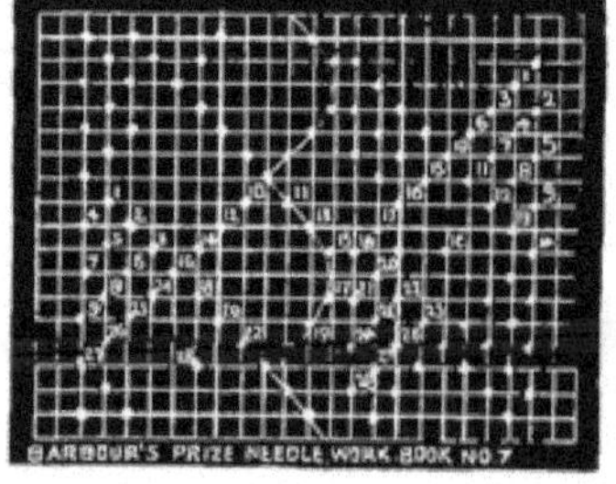

It will be remembered that a pin is always "closed" with the same movement that precedes it unless otherwise specified.

INSERTION.

Materials: Barbour's new Irish flax lace thread, No. 250, 12 pairs bobbins. Pin 3 pairs in 28, 3 in 19, 3 in 14, 1 in 25, 26, and 27.

Open hole ground: Ht 9th and 10th, pin in 1; (a) wt 10th and 11th, 11th and 12th, pin in 2; wt 10th and 11th (a); ht 8th and 9th, pin in 3; ht 9th and 10th, pin in 4; repeat (a) to (a), pin in 5; ht 7th and 8th, pin in 6; ht 8th and 9th, pin in 7; ht 9th and 10th, pin in 8; repeat (a) to (a), putting pin in 9; ht 6th and 7th, pin in 10; ht 7th and 8th, pin in 11; ht 8th and 9th, pin in 12; ht 9th and 10th, pin in 13; repeat (a) to (a), putting pin in 14; ht 5th and 6th. pin in 15; ht 4th and 5th, pin in 16; ht 3d and 4th, pin in 17; (b) wt 2d and 3d, 1st and 2d, pin in 18; wt 2d and 3d (b); tw 4th, 5th, 6th, 7th, 8th, and 9th twice; (c) ctc 6th and 7th, 7th and 8th, 8th and 9th, 5th and 6th, 6th and 7th, 7th and 8th, 4th and 5th, 5th and 6th, 6th and 7th (c), pin in 19; repeat (c) to (c); tw all pairs used in spider 3 times. Ht 3d and 4th, pin in 20; repeat (b) to (b), pin in 21; ht 4th and 5th, pin in 22; 3d and 4th, pin in 23; repeat (b) to (b), putting pin in 24; ht 5th and 6th, pin in 25; ht 4th and 5th, pin in 26; ht 3d and 4th, pin in 27; repeat (b) to (b), putting pin in 28.

The corner is turned as described in No. 5, by working up to a diagonal, tying the threads carefully before the last pins, removing these, pinning in an opposite diagonal one row holes back, and continuing.

The pattern for this lace and insertion is shown on one block, which illustrates also the method of using the checked or quadrille paper in taking off patterns. By means of this a pattern may be enlarged or reduced with perfect accuracy, designs may be copied from lace samples, or originate — which is a most pleasing study. Permit me to say that I received my instruction from Barbour's Prize Needlework Series No. 3 — the first directions I had ever seen, and which are so clear in every particular that I had not the slightest difficulty in following them.

MEXICAN BORDER.

[Contributed by Miss JESSIE D. ROEDEL, 441 Cumberland Street, Lebanon, Pa.]

Materials: Barbour's Irish flax thread, No. 100, 3-cord, 200-yards spools, and square of linen as large as required, medium quality.

Make a 1½-inch hem; draw 6 threads, or more, according to quality of linen. To hemstitch, throw the thread as for a buttonhole st, take up 4 or 6 threads, st through 2 threads down straight to draw it tight. Draw threads, ½ inch wide, and ½ inch from hem for first border. Hemstitch on both sides, doing the work always on the wrong side, buttonhole corners on 2 sides, and wherever the linen is cut. Leave ½ inch plain, * draw space 1/16 inch less than 2

Mexican Border.

inches, leave ½ inch, repeat from *, and draw ½ inch. A description of drawn-work seems quite superfluous, as it is almost universally copied from engravings. This design was copied from a table-cover bought from a Mexican, and is very effective.

DOILY, IN DRAWN-WORK AND CROCHET.

[Contributed by Miss C. S. LEE, 127 Walnut Street, Greenville, Mississippi.]

Materials: One spool each Barbour's Irish flax linen thread, No. 100, No. 70, and No. 30, white, 3-cord, 200-yards spools, linen 8½ inches square, with steel hook, size 00.

Doily, in Drawn-Work and Crochet.

Draw several threads around square 1⅛ inch from edge, and with No. 100 thread hemstitch for fringe, or if preferred, turn hem and hemstitch. The drawn-work extends diagonally across the doily; draw ¼ inch and miss ¼ inch, each way. Leave ¼ inch between this and fringe. Buttonhole with No. 100 thread around the drawn-work, the design for which is so simple as to need no description. Featherstitch around edge of doily, and around the wheel; for this work use No. 30 thread, and for the wheel No. 70. With ⅞-inch staple, make 20 loops, with 3 dc in centre. The description for this work has been so often given that details seem unnecessary. Fasten thread to a loop on one side, run hook through each of 20 loops, pick up thread, and draw through all at once. Fasten securely. Join ends with needle, or sc together.

1. Make 5 dc in each of 20 outer loops, joining last to first with sc.

2. Dc in each dc, widening every 5th st with 2 dc in 1 st; join.

3. Dc in each dc; join.

4. Ch 10, tc in dc directly over loop below, * ch 7, miss 5, tc in next dc, and repeat, joining to 3d of 10 ch.

5. Dc in each tc and each st of ch; join.

6. Dc in dc, widening with 2 dc in centre dc of each ch; join.

Baste the wheel firmly in centre of linen corner, buttonhole securely with No. 100 thread, and cut linen carefully from beneath. The wheel is very delicate in appearance, and would be effectively applied to larger pieces of work, or it may be used for tidies, cushion-covers, etc.

CORNER, IN SWEDISH DRAWN-WORK.

[Contributed by Mrs. Hedvig Muller, New York, N.Y.]

Materials: Barbour's white star flossette, size * * * *, or shade No. 40 Ulster rope linen, 10 skeins, 5 skeins Ulster etching flax, 1 spool Irish flax thread, No. 150, 3-cord, 200-yards spools, and square of scrim 32 × 32 inches.

The design may be readily followed, as the model shows unfinished portions. The squares are formed by drawing ⅓ inch, and leaving ⅓ inch. Work over and under the undrawn thread, dividing them in two parts, using the etching flax for this purpose. The purls in the centre square are made by winding the flax around the needle, and drawing through as in Raleigh bars. The spiders or wheels filling these squares are of the No. 150 thread. The satin-stitch embroidery is of the rope linen, as also are the rows of darning-stitch.

This work is far more quickly accomplished than the ordinary drawn-work, and is not trying to the eyes. The white linen floss

Corner, in Swedish Drawn-work.

washes beautifully, too, and has all the lustre of silk. Scarfs, centre-pieces, etc., are made in this work, always with the utmost satisfaction and pleasure.

SQUARE, IN DRAWN-WORK.

[Contributed by Mrs. S. S. Peniston, Andalusia, Pa.]

Materials: Barbour's Irish flax thread, No. 150, 3-cord, 200-yards spools, and a square of very fine linen.

The stitches are so plainly given that no description is necessary. One-quarter of the square is shown, reduced about two-thirds, but

Square, in Drawn-Work.

may be enlarged as one likes. Many think that threads must be counted, in drawing, but if one tries measuring instead much time and care will be saved.

FIVE O'CLOCK TEA-CLOTH WITH CUT-WORK BORDER.

[Contributed by Mrs. Chas. M. D. Kay, Elliot House, Toronto, Canada.]

Materials: Barbour's Irish flax thread, No. 50, 3-cord, 200-yards spools, and fine butcher's linen, 1¼ yards square. The Ulster etching flax, or white flossette, size 1, may be used for the filling-stitches with excellent effect.

Buttonhole all lines save the veining of the large leaves, which is done in outline stitch. It is an excellent plan, when this can be done, to cut away the linen and fold back to the line which is to be

Five O'clock Tea-cloth with Cut-work Border.

buttonholed over, as described in the Danish antique work, appearing in No. 4, No. 5, and No. 6 of the Prize Needlework Series. Otherwise, when the buttonholing is completed, cut the linen as close as possible without clipping the stitches. Buttonhole the edge of the centre all around and fill in the spiders and twisted bars. A simple but rich and effective design.

SQUARE, IN ROMAN EMBROIDERY.

[Contributed by JULIA D. SMITH, Box 159, West Medway, Mass.]

Materials: Barbour's Irish flax thread, No. 50, 3-cord, 200-yards spools, and 11-inch square of firm butcher's linen. Finer thread and linen may be used if preferred.

Square, in Roman Embroidery.

Trace or stamp the design on the linen, and buttonhole the lines closely. The surface stitches are simple but effective, being the loop or "bird's-eye" stitch, with which all are familiar. Push the needle up through the fabric, then down again in the same place, leaving a loop of requisite length, — say, for this purpose, $\frac{1}{4}$ to $\frac{1}{3}$ inch. Bring the needle up at tip of loop, pass it over the thread and down on the other side, thus making a short stitch to hold the loop in place. In the corner leaves 3 of these loops start from a central point, in the side scrolls they are single. Barbour's Ulster etching flax, cream or white, is used for this work with beautiful effect.

SAILOR COLLAR, IN ROMAN EMBROIDERY.

[Contributed by Mrs. F. P. Bernard, Warren, Minn.]

Materials: Barbour's Irish flax thread, No. 50, 3-cord, 200-yards spools, and ½ yard linen of suitable quality. If preferred, Bar-

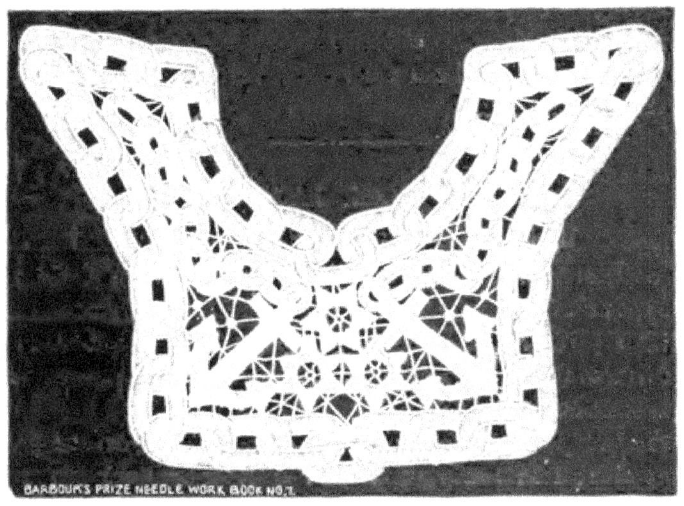

Sailor Collar, in Roman Embroidery.

bour's Ulster etching flax or linen embroidery floss No. 5 for finer work may be used instead of the thread.

Procure a sailor collar of size desired, — that given is large enough for the average child of five years, — fasten the linen to a board with a few pins, place the pattern on this and mark around the edges. Cut a link from some stiff paper, 1¾ × 1⅛ inches, making the opening same width as one side of link, ⅜ inch. The smaller links are 1¼ × ¾ inch, proportioned like the larger ones, the anchors 3½ inches long, and stars 1½ inches from point to point. With the large link pattern begin at the neck and work down to point in front, and around to centre of back; then begin on other side and work around to centre of back in same way, then add the centre links in back of collar, top and bottom. Lay on the star pattern, mark edges and centres, — ⅝ inch, — then the anchors and the small chains. After the lines are all properly marked, trace with a coarse doubled thread, put in the lace-stitches, buttonhole all edges, wash, press dry, and carefully cut out the linen. If you wish your work to look well, do not rub it when washing, but press the dirt out. To iron, have four thicknesses of woolen under the ironing sheet, place the collar right side down, pull into shape, and iron under thin white cloth. After marking out the links it is well to erase the cross lines not intended to be worked, so that no mistake will be made.

WORK BAG.

[Contributed by SATIE J. CAMPIN, Orlando, Florida.]

Materials: Barbour's Ulster etching flax, 2 skeins shade 2, 1 skein each shade ½, 20, and 21, and 1 skein Ulster rope linen, shade 2, with 2 yards No. 2 ribbon, yellow satin, or in accordance with the colors of the floss if other style of decoration is chosen. For the foundation use heavy linen or duck.

Take a strip of the fabric 11 × 21 inches, turn a hem at top 2½ inches wide; take a strip 3½ × 38 inches, for the pockets, turn ½ inch hem; pin this at bottom of wide strip, and between it and the top sketch or stamp sprays of buttercups (or any small flowers), working these in Kensington stitch, shade No. 21 for stems and veining of leaves, No. 20 for leaves and French knots in centres of buttercups, and shades No. ½ and 2 for the flowers. Press and rip the hem at each end, sew these up so it will be finished when the hem is folded back, make a row of featherstitching at foot of hem, using shade No. 2, and another row an inch above, making space to run ribbon in; double the bag, cut a buttonhole in the middle, between the rows of featherstitching, perpendicular, and on outside only, and another on each side of the seam, and run the ribbon in from each side, making the draw-strings. Work the edge of the hem on the long strip as the other, mark the bag in 3-inch spaces at the bottom, seam the ends of the narrow strip and baste on to form pockets, laying a box pleat in the centre of each ; baste down between the pockets, and feather-stitch. Take 2 rounds of pasteboard 7 inches in diameter, cover one side of each with the goods and sew together, turn in lower edge of bag and join to this, twist a cord of the Ulster rope linen, shade No. 2, to cover this joining, and you have as pretty a bag as any one could wish. The etching flax is very nice to work with, having the same gloss as silk, and filling in so much faster than the fine filo. Any colors liked may be used, always doing the featherstitching with the darkest shade in the flowers, and having the ribbon to match. A cross-stitch embroidery would be very pretty for this. These bags sell very readily at fairs, and are nice and useful holiday gifts.

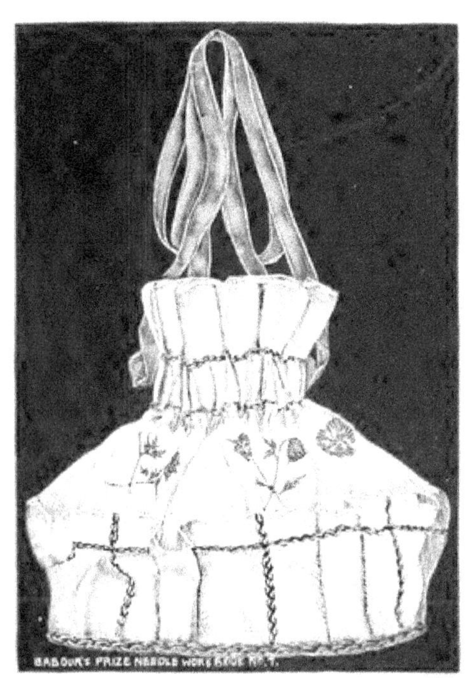

Work Bag.

TABLE COVER.

Materials: Barbour's rope linen, size 00, 7 skeins No. 155, 8 of No. 153, and 3 each of No. ½ and No. 40, with a yard square of heavy linen, unbleached, and pattern stamped or traced.

This design is very rich and effective. Any colors may be chosen for the work, to harmonize with the furnishings of the room where it is to be used. Shades of green and terra-cotta would be specially effective.

Table Cover.

The Ulster rope linen has all the effect of silk, is much less expensive, and far more durable, as it does not roughen and wear off with use. Hence it is especially recommended for real service.

CENTRE-PIECE AND DOILIES — COLONIAL DESIGN.

[Contributed by Mrs. SARAH J. G. SOLLEY, Deerfield, Mass.]

Materials: Barbour's Ulster etching flax, blue, 3 shades, 23-inch square art linen for centre-piece, 6-inch hemstitched squares for doilies. For hemstitching use No. 150 Barbour's Irish flax thread.

The stitches used are simple catstitch, outline, seed, satin, feather, Queen Anne, French knot, etc., and any preferred combination may be affected.

Centre-piece.

The designs are such as were used by Colonial dames in the long ago in a great variety of decoration, before stamping and transfer patterns were thought of. In their origination or adaptation there is opportunity for the display of individual talent, and the study is most interesting. Each design as worked may be sketched with the

Doilies.

pencil, care being taken to produce a general harmony of effect; and the work is not confined to doilies and centre-pieces, but is especially adapted to the decoration of large pieces, such as counterpanes, table-covers, etc., using the Ulster rope linen for the heavier embroidery, and No. 8 floss for very fine work.

Any arrangement of stitches is permissible, and in their variation and the origination of new and quaint designs the interested needle-worker will find a source of continued interest and pleasure.

SOFA-PILLOW, IN OUTLINE AND CROSS-STITCH EMBROIDERY.

[Contributed by JULIA D. SMITH, Box 159, W. Medway, Mass.]

Materials: Barbour's Ulster rope linen, shades Nos. 151, 153, and 155, 2 skeins each, with square of ecru canvas having design stamped or traced. If preferred to the cord, the edge may be finished with a frill of ribbon or china silk, matching either shade of floss.

Sofa-Pillow in Outline and Cross-Stitch Embroidery.

Other shades of floss may be chosen, in harmony with the furnishings of the room. Shades Nos. 43, 121, and 122, used together, are very effective, or shades Nos. 131, 132, and 136.

SOFA PILLOW.

[Contributed by Miss A. M. Fitch, 58 Olive Street, New Haven, Conn.]

Materials: Barbour's Irish flax thread, No. 25, 3-cord, 200-yards spools, white star flossette, size *, a piece of rick-rack braid, and

Sofa Pillow.

square of denim, any preferred color. For tacking on the braid use the spool linen, taking a stitch in every point. The fancy stitches are done with the flossette, and may be varied to suit the taste of the worker. Around the braid on the outer edge of design is a row of buttonhole stitches, short and long alternating. The half-ovals in the corners are outlined with featherstitching, the lower being filled with honeycomb stitch — an open buttonhole stitch caught into loop of preceding row — and surrounded by "rays," in satin-stitch. The bars or spokes extending toward the centre from the inner row of rick-rack are simple chain-stitch, and the combination, while of the plainest description as to stitches, is greatly admired. It may be utilized on nearly any design for sofa pillows and table-covers in colored denim, or on white linen for table service, with most satisfactory results. The model is all in white, but if preferred the Ulster rope linen in colors may be used in one or more shades, combined with the rick-rack, and if a heavier effect is desired the Ulster braid may be substituted for this with great satisfaction. The making of pillows has no end, and many simple, charming designs are easily evolved if one has at hand suitable material, with the Ulster rope linen. Work done with this floss is serviceable as well as pretty. Another pillow easily made was on red and white checked gingham, the red crossed with white, lined with denim of red and white mixed, the ruffle hem being turned over from the wrong side and feather-stitched with white. Still another was of denim, checked off in inch spaces diagonally (beginning at a corner), these lines outlined in plain or knotted stitch (see page 73, Barbour's Prize Needlework Series, No. 6), and a little star of crossed threads put in the intersections. For these stars different colors may be used with good effect, serving to use up any odd bits of the rope linen floss you may have remaining from various pieces of work.

FLEUR-DE-LIS DOILY.

[Contributed by Miss Alice Luka, Van Deusen, Mass.]

Materials: Barbour's Ulster etching flax, 2 skeins each shade No. 151, 153, and 154, and 1 skein No. 156, with square of linen 13 × 13 inches.

Trace or stamp the pattern. Buttonhole the point of the fleur-de-lis with shade No. 151, outlining remainder, and filling in with

Fleur-de-Lis Doily.

any fancy stitches that may suggest themselves. The leaves of alternate figures are treated in the same way, with No. 153 and 154, and the bands are of No. 156. This piece is easily made, and has been greatly admired.

SQUARE FOR SMALL TABLE.

[Contributed by Miss ELLEN MULLER, New York, N.Y.]

Materials: Barbour's Ulster etching flax, 2 skeins each shade Nos. 52 and 53, and square of rather heavy linen 16 × 16 inches. Any shades that are liked may be chosen instead of those given.

Allowing ¾ inch for the hem, draw ¼ inch 1½ inches from the edge, miss ⅛ inch, draw ¼ inch. Hemstitch this with No. 52, crossing the thread over the plain space as it is carried from one side to the other in taking up the threads. This method of hemstitching with color is very effective. The embroidery is done with outline, satin, feather, bird's-eye, cross-stitch, etc., and any fancy

Square for Small Table.

stitches may be introduced that, according to the worker's idea, will add to the effect sought. While apparently elaborate, this work is very simple and offers opportunity for much originality.

SOFA PILLOW.

[Contributed by Miss C. B. FITCH, 58 Olive Street, New Haven, Conn.]

Materials: Barbour's white flossette, size **, new Ulster braid, and square of denim, 18 × 18 inches, or size desired.

Sofa Pillow.

Block off the denim in squares of 3 inches, basting on the braid. To fasten, in every 3d loop on the edge of the braid make 2 short stitches, with a long stitch between, using the white flossette for this purpose. The effect is in every way equal to silk, and it is far more suitable for such use. The design in the centre of each square is made by using a ring of the flossette, winding it 8 or 10 times around a small cork ½ inch in diameter, and buttonholing over the loop closely all around. In the centre of each ring is a star of crossed threads, and at even distances around it groups of 5 stitches, graduated in length. The ruffle is finished with a row of buttonhole or blanket stitches, 2 short, ¼ inch apart, then 3 as described in applying the braid. The whole effect, although so simple a design, is very charming.

The same idea may be carried out as a border for a table-cover, scarf, portière, etc., making a row of squares all around, with blocks in the corners, or as liked. It is effective, not only on colored denims, but on white linen.

If preferred, the ruffle of the pillow may be edged with the braid, applied as described. Other designs, such as are suitable for centre-pieces of braid, may be used instead of the simple blocking. On page 72, book No. 6 of Barbour's Prize Needlework Series, is a Russian centre-piece, the single figures of which are extremely unique applied to the centre of such a pillow.

CENTRE-PIECE, IN CROSS-STITCH.

[Contributed by HATTIE D. ROCKWELL, 44 Thwing Street, Boston, Mass.]

Materials: Barbour's Ulster etching flax, light, medium, and dark blue, or as shown in illustration, "Deerfield" shades, 2 skeins light, 1 skein each medium and dark, and pattern stamped on 12-inch square of round-thread linen.

Use the light shade for buttonholing the edge, the dark for the single crosses, or outline of the pattern, and the medium for the remainder. Or vary this arrangement in any way to suit the taste. Other colors may be chosen instead of the blue. Shades No. 70, No. 71, and No. 20 combine beautifully, also shades No. 30, No. 30½, and No. 82. This class of work is much more artistic than Kensington embroidery, unless properly done, and the merest novice in needlework will be able to make an entire success of it. Odds and ends of the Ulster etching flax may be used very effectively in cross-stitching, care being taken to combine the colors harmoni-

Centre-piece, in Cross-stitch.

ously. This embroidery material will be found lustrous, durable, and far less expensive than silk.

PHOTOGRAPH FRAMES.

[Contributed by Miss M. C. PARSONS, 526 State Street, Hudson, N.Y.]

Materials: Barbour's Irish flax thread No. 90, with No. 50 for rings, 3-cord, 200-yards spools, 8 yards linen braid, 5 yards purling, and ½ yard yellow satin.

For the larger frame cut a piece of heavy pasteboard, 8½ × 10 inches, cut an oval opening in the centre 4½ × 3½ inches, place over one side a layer of wadding, cover with satin, and glue down well at the back. For the opening, cut the satin out toward the edge and fold to the back smoothly. For the back cut a piece of pasteboard ¼ inch smaller all around, cover with the satin, or with

Photograph Frame.

cotton surah of same shade, and fasten firmly to the front all around, leaving space to slip the picture in at top or bottom. Attach to the back a strip of heavy pasteboard, covered, as a standard, or a wire support, if preferred. When complete, the bit of lace is fastened in place, caught on with slight stitches so as to be readily removed. For this 4½ yards of braid are required.

Photograph Frame.

The smaller frame is, outside, 8 × 8 inches, but may be made longer than wide if preferred. Cut the oblong opening 3⅜ × 2¾ inches. Take ¼ yard of satin, cut lengthwise, join ends, and fasten around inner and outer edges, having most of the fulness come at the corners. Tack this to form puffs, finish as directed for larger frame, and fasten the lace square lightly in place; 3½ yards of braid for this, 12 small rings and 4 larger ones. For the large frame, 4 small rings, 12 of next size, and 2 of next are wanted.

Any pretty designs for doilies may be utilized in making these frames, and when one tires of them they may be again put to the original purpose. They are quickly made, and sell wonderfully well at bazaars, where "something new" is always the demand. Let me say that Barbour's Irish flax thread No. 90 is used by me for fine Renaissance or Battenburg lace-work in preference to any other make.

CURTAINS, WITH RENAISSANCE LACE AND INSERTION.

[Contributed by Mrs. H. D. PLANT, 130 Van Buren Street, Brooklyn, N.Y.]

Materials: Barbour's Irish flax thread, 20 spools No. 50 and 8 spools of No. 25, 3-cord, 200-yards spools, 108 yards of wide hemstitch braid, and 432 yards of narrow, with 14 yards of linen scrim.

This design is entirely original, and very rich in effect. The materials given are for two pairs of curtains. No. 25 thread is used for making the rings, 3,000 in number, the larger ones wound over a smooth stick 5/8 inch in diameter, the smaller ones over a pencil. There is no difficulty in making rings rapidly and well, and the effect is far superior to that given by the rings which are purchased ready-made. No. 50 thread is used for whipping the braid and for the filling stitches.

The edge of curtains is composed of two leaves filled in with point de Venise and point de Bruxelles. The circular figures are made with a ring in the centre, fastened with plain twisted (Sorrento) bars, and the spaces between are filled with spiders. The edge is 3 inches in width, and the wide braid is used on the straight side.

The insertion is 10 inches wide, or nearly so, and corresponds with the edge, the five upper leaves of the main figure being filled alternately with the same stitches, which may, of course, be varied and made more or less elaborate to please one's fancy. The scrolls

Curtains, with Renaissance Lace and Insertion.

on each side are filled with 9 rings and plain cross-stitch; inside the scrolls are two figures composed of five circles, each filled with bars fastened in the centre with a buttonhole stitch. All other spaces are filled with spiders varying in size to fit the space.

On either side of the scroll figure is a band designed to make the curtain hang straight and prevent the sagging which is so often seen in draperies made with this work. This is worked with rings and fastened with bars.

The simple drawn-work insertion adds to the beauty of this design. This is so easy as to need no description. The rows of double-hemstitching are ½ inch in width, requiring the drawing of 8 or 10 threads, the wheel pattern twice that width. The threads are knotted in clusters of 4 threads each, 6 of these being drawn together with a wheel darned around, using for this 4 threads drawn from the scrim.

In conclusion, I am sure no lady will have any difficulty in following this design, having a section of the pattern in lace and insertion with the corner; and I may add that having used Barbour's Irish flax thread for this class of work, no one will take any other. It is not only less expensive than the so-called Battenburg thread, but vastly superior.

INFANT'S PILLOW.

[Contributed by Mrs. GWEN KEYS, 1103 Corning Street, Red Oak, Iowa.]

Materials: Barbour's Irish flax thread, No. 80, 3-cord, 200-yards spools, white, ¾ yard fine lawn, 2 yards honiton leaf braid, medium size, and 10 yards baby ribbon, color desired.

The pillow, without ruffle, is 14 × 11 inches, and the ruffle is 2½ inches deep. Trace the design for embroidery, and baste on the medallions carefully, then buttonhole around each with the thread, 1 long and 2 short st. Cut the lawn from beneath the braid, taking care not to clip the embroidery. Finish the ruffle for each side separately, making a narrow hem, hemstitched with the thread, then draw enough threads above the hem to run the ribbon in. The ruffle should be full enough to go twice across before it is gathered. The ends are tapered to each corner, the ribbon run through spaces and made in a bow at corners, and the cushion

Infant's Pillow.

should match the ribbon in color. The model is pink, but blue or lavender would be very pretty. If preferred, the Ulster etching flax may be used for the buttonholing. This has a lustre equal to silk, and washes well. The thread, however, is delicate in appearance, and also lustrous.

RUSSIAN CENTRE-PIECE.

[Contributed by Mrs. HEDVIG MULLER, New York, N.Y.]

Materials: Three spools Barbour's Irish flax thread, No. 35, 3-cord, 200-yards spools, 1 spool No. 100 same linen, for whipping curves, 16-inch square of linen, and 24 yards new Ulster braid.

Russian Centre-piece.

The design and stitches are so clearly shown as to require no further explanation. The centre-piece, complete, is 22 inches square, and an extremely effective bit of work. This braid, of pure linen with a cord running through the centre, is very ornamental in itself, and only the simplest stitches are required to bring it out. A pattern in which the braid need not be turned is necessary, but very many Battenburg patterns may be adapted to it, and some especially beautiful designs have appeared in previous books. Hold the braid firmly to the pattern with the thumb and forefinger of one hand, shaping it to the angle or curve with the other, then baste securely in place.

YOKE, IN RENAISSANCE LACE.

[Contributed by Mrs. W. M. WEEKS, Lyndonville, Vermont.]

Materials: Barbour's Irish flax thread, No. 100 and No. 60, 3-cord, 200-yards spools, with 7 yards of linen hemstitch braid, cream, gray, or white, as preferred.

Yoke, in Renaissance Lace.

The design is a simple but very effective one, intended for the front of a dress-yoke. It may be duplicated for the back, if desired, and the two leaves, five-petalled, at the sides used for collar ornaments with fine effect. The stitches are not elaborate, and require no description. Ladies will find Barbour's Irish flax thread as superior for this class of lace-making as for others.

LADY'S CORSAGE COLLAR.

[Contributed by LUELLA C. HOLZAPFEL, Oklahoma City, Okla.]

Materials: Two spools Barbour's Irish flax lace thread, No. 250, 2-cord, 200-yards spools (or No. 150, if preferred), 36 yards plain point lace braid, and 5 yards purling.

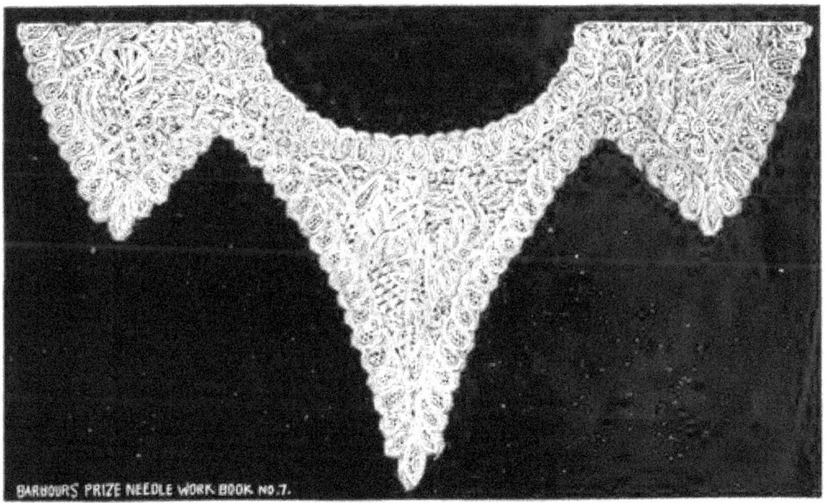

Lady's Corsage Collar.

Follow directions given in No. 6 for basting braid, etc. In the model, the fan lace-stitch is used as a ground-work, but this may very effectively be chosen as a filling-in stitch for the design, the ground-work being more open. The collar fastens on left shoulder, the points reaching the waist-line at front and back, and the square tabs falling over the shoulders.

DRESSER SCARF, IN ROYAL BATTENBURG.

[Contributed by JESSIE D. ROEDEL, 441 Cumberland Street, Lebanon, Pa.]

Materials: Barbour's Irish flax thread, 1 spool No. 150, 3 spools No. 100, and 2 spools No. 80, 3-cord, 200-yards spools, 26 yards of

linen hemstitch braid, 5 yards of purling, and a strip of linen, length and width desired for dresser, say 18 × 45 inches. Hemstitch this 1 inch wide on one edge. Stitches are much the same as described in "Square with Battenburg Lace," page 85, No. 6. This scarf may be lengthened by adding another side figure, and the design is very handsome used as a border for tea-cloth. As a lace-worker of many years, my testimony in regard to the excellence of Barbour's Irish flax thread, for lace-making, may not be without value. Having used this thread in every branch of the work, I can heartily recommend it. In this piece use No. 150 for hemstitching the fabric and for whipping curves, felling angles, etc., No. 100 for the groundwork of Venetian bars, also for the closest filling stitches, and No. 80 for rosette (point d'Angleterre) stitch, and others similar.

POINT LACE HANDKERCHIEFS.

HANDKERCHIEF NO. 1.

[Contributed by Mrs. J. Moore, Stoughton, Mass.]

Materials: Barbour's Irish flax lace thread, No. 250, 2-cord, 200-yards spools, 7 yards purling, 1 yard each of two fancy braids, and ¾ yard honiton medallion.

The purling is used to render dainty work, and the whole should be done with the No. 250 thread, which is smooth, lustrous, and strong enough to make good, durable work. After the purling is whipped to fit the pattern perfectly, the circles are filled with "spider-web" stitch, for which directions are accurately given in No. 5 and No. 6 of Barbour's Prize Needlework Series. The plain row of braid next the edge is joined with point d'Anvers stitch. The filling is in imitation of real fish-net, and is done double, the thread being stretched as evenly as possible from point to point and twisted back; this runs all one way. Stretch threads across these to form perfect squares, and in twisting back make 3 twists between crossings and fasten with 3 buttonhole stitches drawn tight enough to form a strong knot. Finish the edge with another row of purling. I find if the purling is held from right to left and the needle carried

Point Lace Handkerchiefs.

a little aslant towards the left, catching enough of the purling, it does not require whipping, and time is saved. As a teacher and lace-maker of many years' experience, I wish to say that Barbour's Irish flax threads are the most satisfactory I ever used. For fine work No. 250 cannot be excelled, whether for lace work or very dainty plain sewing; for hemming or hemstitching fine lawn it cannot be excelled.

HANDKERCHIEF NO. 2.

[Contributed by KATHARINE G. GROVE, Lancaster, Pa.]

Materials: Barbour's Irish flax lace thread, No. 250, 2-cord, 200-yards spools, 3½ yards plain point lace braid, 1 yard purling, and 12-inch square of fine linen lawn.

Only a corner pattern is needed. Baste braid and proceed with stitches as directed in Book No. 6. The sides of the square are hemstitched, and the lace-corners neatly felled in place. The design is very simple and easy of accomplishment, yet the effect is decidedly charming as well as novel.

HANDKERCHIEFS NOS. 3 AND 4.

[Contributed by Mrs. L. A. THOMPSON, 2512 Irving Street, Denver, Col.]

Materials for No. 3: One spool Barbour's Irish flax lace thread, No. 250, 2-cord, 200-yards spools, 7 yards plain point lace braid, 2 yards purling, ⅓ yard honiton medallions, and 12-inch square of linen lawn. Materials for No. 4 are the same, omitting the medallions, and using one yard more of point lace braid.

These designs, while as dainty in effect as can be imagined, are very simple, and a pattern may be easily made from the illustrations. The stitches are of the plainest description, consisting of twisted or Sorrento bars, "spiders" and, in the corner spaces of No. 3, plain buttonhole stitch, or point de Bruxelles. The corner of the latter handkerchief makes a beautiful collar-point.

I wish to urge all ladies who make fine laces to try the new lace thread, No. 250. It works beautifully, and having tested its merits I am sure its use will be continued.

Renaissance Lace Centre-piece.

RENAISSANCE LACE CENTRE-PIECE.

[Contributed by Miss M. C. PARSONS, Hudson, N.Y.]

Materials: Six spools Barbour's Irish flax thread, No. 50, 3-cord, 200-yards spools, 18 yards linen hemstitch braid, 4 yards purling, and 6-inch square of linen for centre.

Make the rings by winding thread 10 times around a pencil and buttonholing over. The design is not intricate, and the stitches are very simple, composed entirely of twisted bars and plain wheels, yet the effect is very lovely. The centre, leaving off the first straight row of braid with remainder of pattern, makes a very pretty little doily.

POINT LACE FAN.

[Contributed by ELLA BOTTORFF, Corydon, Indiana.]

Materials: Barbour's new Irish flax lace thread, No. 250, 2-cord, 200-yards spools, 11 yards of plain point lace braid, and 2 yards of purling.

The border alone makes a lovely edge for handkerchief, and the entire design, omitting the ends of border, may be duplicated to form a doily, having a linen centre. Medallions formed of the

Point Lace Fan.

narrow braid, as shown, and filled with lace-stitches, are much more effective than medallions which are purchased by the yard. The filling stitches are varied, and Raleigh bars are used as a groundwork throughout, giving the work an exquisitely dainty while substantial crisp appearance. For such lace-making the new lace thread referred to cannot be surpassed.

DRESS FRONT, IN BATTENBURG LACE.

[Contributed by Miss FLORA KINGSLEY, Mansfield, Pa.]

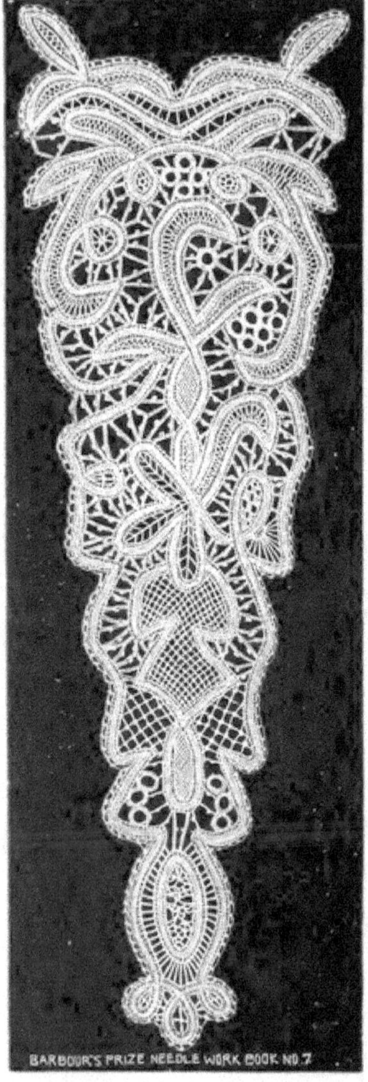

Dress Front, in Battenburg Lace.

Materials: Barbour's Irish flax thread, 1 spool each of No. 100 and No. 150, and 6 yards of linen hemstitch braid, narrow width.

Use No. 150 for whipping curves and felling angles, and No. 100 for rings and lace-stitches. For the rings, wind thread 6 times around a pencil, slip off, and buttonhole over. The stitches are so clearly shown that no description is necessary, particularly as this has been given in No. 5 and No. 6. The loop, between groups of 3 rings, is filled with cloth or darning stitch and the space just above with plain point de Bruselles. Outside this are the buttonhole or Raleigh bars, and below the net stitch, which is especially effective for large spaces. Carry the thread from point to point across, at even distances, and all one way, twisting back on each thread and whipping along the edge of the braid to next point; ¼ inch is a good distance for ordinary work.

As a lace-maker of much experience, I may say that I consider Barbour's Irish flax threads, in the various numbers, superior for this work.

Rose Doily.

ROSE DOILY.

[Contributed by ERMELINDA C. NOBLE, Anniston, Ala.]

Materials: Barbour's Irish flax lace thread, No. 250, 2-cord, 200-yards spools, 7 yards plain point lace braid, 1½ yards purling, and 5-inch square of fine linen lawn.

Description of work is unnecessary, as full directions have so often been given in the Prize Needlework Series, notably in Nos. 5

and 6. This design may be adapted very readily to a handkerchief by adding one or more side figures, according to size desired. For use as a doily, many will prefer to use Barbour's Irish flax thread, No. 150, 3-cord, 200-yards spools. No. 250 is about equal to the ordinary No. 1200 thread, but is a pure linen and works beautifully. This doily is extremely dainty, and suitable for holding a rose-bowl especially.

HANDKERCHIEF, IN THREAD LACE.

[Contributed by Mrs. MARY J. CLARKE, 1408 E. Spruce Street, Seattle, Wash.]

Materials: Two spools Barbour's Irish flax lace thread, No. 250, 2-cord, 200-yards spools, 1 spool No. 120 Irish flax thread, 3-cord, 200-yards spools, 5-inch square of linen lawn, and crochet hook, size 000.

Draw the design on tracing linen, or procure the stamped pattern, if preferred, hem the linen narrowly and baste in centre of pattern, crochet 24 yards of chain, using the No. 120 linen for this, baste this firmly on the design, and fill in with lace-stitches, as shown, or any others that are liked. If preferred, braid may be used instead of the crocheted cord, but I am sure that any who try this method will be pleased. It is real thread lace, and has a dainty crispness hard to imitate. Any figures may be traced, outlined with the cord and filled in, then applied to collars, handkerchief borders, etc.

RENAISSANCE CENTRE-PIECE.

[Contributed by Mrs. W. E. Scott, 270 W. 119th Street, New York, N.Y.]

Materials: Barbour's Irish flax thread, No. 50, 3-cord, 200-yards spools, and 10 yards linen hemstitch braid. Six spools of thread will be sufficient for rings and work.

Follow directions given in No. 6 Book for basting braid, whipping curves, etc. For the large rings, 32 in number, wind thread 20 times around a stick ½ inch in diameter, slip off, and buttonhole over; for the smaller rings use a pencil, and wind 12 times. The bars are heavier than usual, the thread being carried twice across, and twisted over closely. The ordinary tc in crocheting may be used, putting thread over as many times as length of space demands. Crocheted and tatted wheels are used most effectively in this class of work, either in coarse or fine thread. Other stitches require no description. The purling is crocheted: Fasten in a picot of braid, * ch 3, miss 2, 1 dc in next picot, and repeat. Next row is the same, fastening under 3 ch of previous row. This purling is effective and very durable.

The large rings are finished with a tiny spider, woven over crossed threads, in the centre. These rings may be purchased, or are easily made, and are very rich looking. Fasten the thread in at one side, pushing the needle straight through the ring, twist back, push the needle through and bring it out ¼ the space from last fastening, carry it across the first thread, passing between the twists, fasten opposite, twist back to the centre, make a small wheel or spider

Renaissance Centre-piece.

by weaving the thread around the crossed threads two or three times, then twist out on the single thread to the edge of the ring and fasten. Let me say that, when making spiders or other woven stitches, it is a good plan to hold them down tight with the thumb when drawing up the thread, in order to keep them flat, or prevent them puckering or "bunching up."

Ask for
Barbour's

Established
1784.

It is the best for all uses.
Insist upon having it.
Sold everywhere.

See that the threads you purchase bear labels similar to the following.
THEY ARE STANDARD.

3-CORD 200 YARDS SPOOL THREAD.

TOP LABEL.

IN

DARK BLUE, for strong Sewing

WHITE,
WD. BROWN, (Ecru.)
DRABS,

For Lace Making and Needlework.

REVERSE LABEL.

BALL THREAD.

COLORS.

Grey, White & Ecru.
1 Oz. Balls.

SIZES.

Nos. 16 to 70.
(No. 70 Fine Size.)

LINEN FLOSSES
In all the Art Shades.

ULSTER
ROPE LINEN FLOSS.
THE BARBOUR BROTHERS CO.
NEW YORK.
SIZE 00
SHADE
No 3

Size 00, "Rope," Medium.
" 4, "Etching," Fine.
White Flossette, * ** *** ****
Fine to Coarse.

BARBOUR'S STANDARD
3-Cord Carpet Thread.

BARBOURS' IRISH FLAX.

IN ALL COLORS.

Ask for
Barbour's

Established 1784.

Barbour's Irish Flax Threads

Are made for every branch of trade, and for every purpose where Linen Threads are used.

They are specially adapted and are standard and the best for all kinds of hand sewing and machine work.

LINEN THREADS SPECIALLY MADE FOR

Boot and Shoe Making,
Clothing Manufacturers,
Carpet Sewing,
Harness and Saddlery Making,
Book Binding,
Glove Making,
Fish Nets.

For Strength and Durability

BARBOUR'S
IRISH LINEN THREAD

Is the best for all uses.

Received Highest Awards at World's Fair, Chicago, 1893.

Special Merits.

Distinguished Excellence.
Uniformity.
Strength.
Adaptability.
Durability.

Barbour's Threads receive Highest Awards wherever exhibited.

Spool, Ball, and Skein Threads

IN
ALL
COLORS

For all kinds of coarse, strong sewing, and fine stitching, and for every kind of Art Needlework with Linen.

For sale by all wholesale dry goods jobbing houses, shoe findings and saddlery hardware dealers throughout the country.

At retail by all small-ware dealers, general stores, carpet houses, and shoe findings dealers.

Ask for
BARBOUR'S

Barbour's Ulster Rope Linen Floss

is continually and rapidly advancing in popularity as its perfect adaptability to the varied uses of expensive silks becomes more strongly attested. Its smoothness and lustre is unsurpassed. It is especially adapted for Embroidery, for the decoration of a thousand and one articles for home use and adornment, and with equally as charming effect can be applied as readily to the uses of Knotting, Netting, Knitting, Crocheting, and kindred arts. For Slippers, Mittens, Purses, etc., it is durable, lustrous, firm, and far less expensive than silk, and its sale in this new field is constantly increasing.

75 shades are now on the market, including the Newest Art Shades, and the old favorites: others will be added as approved.

To Wash Embroidery

Make a light suds with Ivory or other pure soap, and (particularly for the first laundering) cool water. Wash one article at a time, finishing with this before taking another. Do not rub the embroidery, or put soap directly upon it. Rinse carefully and quickly in clear, cold water, to which a little salt may be added. After rinsing, place between two thick towels, or in one which may be folded over, roll up, squeeze (in order to extract the moisture), then unroll, place right side down on a soft cloth or flannel folded in several thicknesses, lay a white cloth over the wrong side, and press until dry with a moderately hot iron.

Art Embroidery must be washed with great care

BARBOUR'S
Linen
Thread

www.ingramcontent.com/pod-product-compliance
Lightning Source LLC
Chambersburg PA
CBHW030543270326
41927CB00008B/1493

* 9 7 8 3 7 4 4 7 3 8 1 0 1 *